MW01060692

Understanding & Healing

Codependency

with *Gospel Principles*

By

JOHN C. TURPIN

Copyright © 1992 John C. Turpin
All Rights Reserved

Covenant Communications, Inc.
American Fork, Utah

Printed in the United States of America
First Printing: August 1992
94 95 96 97   10 9 8 7 6 5 4 3 2

*Understanding and Healing Codependency
with Gospel Principles*
ISBN 1–55503–401–2
Library of Congress Catalog Card Number: 92–071901

To my noncodependent wife, Barbara, and our children:
Mike, Jeni, and Laura

Audio Tapes by the Author

Stress Reduction for Mormons
Using Gospel Principles to Overcome Codependency
Healing Codependency with Gospel Principles

Books by the Author

A Positive Approach to Personal Growth
The New Stress Reduction for Mormons

Acknowledgments

I want to acknowledge the help of many people in writing this book. This book would not have been possible without the assistance of Dianne Rasi-Koskinen whose unwavering dedication to a project she believes in and whose typing assitance enabled me to meet deadlines that otherwise would not have been met. Also to Darla Hanks Isackson, Editor at Covenant Communications whose suggestions, editing, and support have made this book a more quality product. I am also thankful to C. Kay Allen, of Denver Colorado for his willingness (for many years) to allow me to use his ideas on the communication model and on ways to deal with anger, apathy, and copouts in more healthy, Christlike ways.

Many of the ideas in this book such as the codependency continuum have come as I have sought the Lord's help to better understand how to help members of the Church deal with their own codependency and to learn how to give more Christlike service to others. I am very thankful for the Lord's help and support. Other ideas have been developed over the years from sources such as talks and lectures, and some of these sources are unknown.

This book is written to provide information on how to recognize and deal with codependency and how to learn to experience healing by learning to provide Christlike service. The information is provided for information purposes only to motive the reader to live the gospel of Jesus Christ more fully, and with the understanding that the readers are at various stages of codependency, and that outside help may be required for some to understand and learn to apply some of its concepts.

The most important thing in life is to live so we can be and remain clean and pure from all sin through the atonement. This means that the Atonement of the Savior becomes the center of our life which enables us to repent of past sins and strive to be clean, today. By living this gospel teaching, we can have peace through applying the scriptures in our lives along with prayer and fasting. This process is the most effective means of dealing with and healing codependency. Whatever you learn in this book to reduce your codependency will be much more helpful to you if you use the principles of the Atonement of the Savior as your foundation.

If you apply the teachings of this book, with the scriptural foundation, then you will find peace and the joy that comes from Christlike service, for the Savior taught we can have peace within no matter what happens in our external world. (John 14.) The concepts in this book are supplementary to the work of the Lord Jesus Christ, and his Church.

This book will point out scriptures which may have been previously overlooked as we strive to understand and heal codependency. The book makes no promises; however, I hope it will help you learn how to deal better with influences in your life which have contributed to your codependency, such as dealing with abuse or being raised in a dysfunctional family.

I love to serve by speaking to the Saints. For many years I have enjoyed speaking at numerous BYU Education Weeks and Know Your Religion Seminars across the United States. I would be glad to come to your ward or stake if it can be arranged.

I would also like to make a request for feedback: Please let me know if this book has helped your journey through life. My home address is 1825 E. Faunsdale Drive, Sandy, Utah 84092. My phone number is 801-572-0304.

SUGGESTED READINGS

The New Stress Reduction for Mormons—a Gospel Journey with 15 Stress Reducing Chapters, Turpin, John C.

Geting What You Want in Life . . . Without Feeling Guilty
Pool, Eliason, Christopherson, workbook

Hold on to Hope—A Spiritual Look At Chemical Addiction and Recovery—A Question of Choice. Lorien Productions 1991. P.O. Box 39 Bountiful, Utah 84011 Video tape

On New Wings: Mormon Women Rediscover Personal Agency and Conquer Codependency, Newbold, Gail

How to Qualify for the Celestial Kingdom Today, Cox, James B.

The following by C. Kay Allen—available through him at:
3835 S. Niagra Way Denver, Colorado 80237. Phone 303-759-2955.

✓ *Developing the Power of Self Control*
workbook

Improving Performance Through Trust and Commitment
workbook

Workbook: A Self-management Seminar

Motivation & Cooperation
workbook

Developing Relationships of Trust and Respect
workbook

✓ *Journey from Fear to Love*
book

The Ways and Power of Love
book (Published by Covenant, 1992. Available in bookstores)

✓ *Beyond Coping—Skills that Make Relationships Work*, Allen, C. Kay
(6-hour tape set)

✓ *Making Things Happen*, Allen, Roger
(6-hour tape set)

TABLE OF CONTENTS

Chapter 1

What Is Codependency?
How Can I Identify Where I Am
on the Codependency Continuum?

It was a bad day for one third grade teacher, mostly because of a little boy who kept getting into mischief. After school as she was about to leave her classroom, she noticed a folded note on her desk. The words on the outside of the note scribbled by the boy read, "To be opened after 4:10."

The time was right, so she opened the note. It read, "I have had a hard life, and you are not making it any easier."

This boy's note illustrates the feelings of most codependents. They think life is hard for them and that it is usually someone else's fault. There is a need to learn more about understanding and healing codependency, for codependency does make life hard. However, life does not need to stay as hard as it is. It can be better.

Christlike service, for instance, makes life rewarding. Codependency motivates a person to give counterfeit service, and just like counterfeit money, counterfeit service makes life harder. Sometimes, though, it is hard to tell the difference between the real and the counterfeit. This book and the three audio tapes, *Using Gospel Principles to Overcome Codependency*, *Healing Codependency wth Gospel Principles*, and *Stress Reduction for Mormons* are provided to make life easier for those who are codependent.

While counseling and traditional books on codependency can be very helpful, these should supplement, not replace, the gospel healing of codependency. In order to be healed, we need to apply the gospel of Jesus Christ in our lives. This book is not a traditional or therapeutic approach to healing codependency. It teaches a gospel-based approach to help you understand codependency and to learn how to heal its negative influence on your life.

While life is hard for all of us at times, we make life harder by our sins, mistakes, weaknesses, and carnal desires. As we become more aware of ways we make our lives hard, we can modify our behaviors so our lives become easier.

LIFE HAS ALSO BEEN HARD FOR OTHERS

One of the major causes of codependent behavior is having a close family member behave very differently than we desire. The temptation is to focus on that person's problems, try to "fix him, " take responsibility for him, and sometimes feel terribly inadequate and guilty because "his behavior must be our fault."

However, the scriptures give us examples of people who responded in a healthy way, even though the behavior of their family members was not desirable. For instance, Father Adam had many children, but one child, Cain, murdered his brother. Even though he had a child who failed miserably, Father Adam continued to serve his Heavenly Father and bless the lives of his children and family. We could assume he responded to this family crisis by getting beyond the need for Cain to meet his expectations (codependency) and past the inappropriate guilt which could have destroyed his ability to serve the Lord and bless his family. We learn from Adam that we can deal with tragedies in our lives in ways that bless our own lives as well as the lives of others.

Abraham's father worshiped idols. Abraham did everything he could do to help his father get his life in order, but Abraham never succeeded. In spite of the failure of his own father, Abraham continued to be one of the great servants of the Lord. We learn from Abraham how to survive even when our own parents have failed us.

Alma's son, Corianton, had so many problems that he obstructed the work of the Lord. By using the experience he gained through struggles earlier in his life, Alma taught his son and exercised his faith in a way that helped him recover and to serve in the ministry. We learn from Alma how to continue to serve the Lord even when our children are failing us. We also learn to never give up on them.

Nephi's struggles with his brothers are well known to us. Could he have been so successful in serving the Lord and his people if he had given in to a codependent need to fix or control Laman and Lemuel? We learn from Nephi to stay close to the Lord and ask for his help even when our own siblings have failed us.

We can learn to give Christlike love and service with an inner strength that helps others without allowing ourselves to be taken advantage of inappropriately. This book can provide help in achieving this goal. Each of us can learn to serve like these scriptural heroes did without codependency, and we can learn to serve the Lord even when those we love or need the most are failing.

WHY CODEPENDENCY MAKES LIFE HARD

Codependency happens when a person needs others too much—so much that this need makes life hard. We all want others to need, appreciate, and love us. That is normal and okay. If instead of only wanting, we compulsively need others to need, appreciate, and love us, this unhealthy need can motivate us to relate to others in an all-consuming way. This unhealthy need makes us willing to do what other people want, even when we know it is not good for us, and even if we know it is a sin. "Codependency is an addiction to people—especially to unhealthy people—in an unhealthy way" (Dave Featherstone). We are codependent when we need others so much that we rescue them from the consequences of their own behavior. Paul Dunn said, "In our desires to help someone in the worst way, sometimes that is exactly what we do." Need for the approval of another person can be so strong that life, self-esteem and self-worth revolve around what another person thinks of us. As a result, we are usually trying to work out another person's salvation over our own. This makes us vulnerable to control and mistreatment from others.

Before the word was ever invented, the Prophet Joseph Smith warned against behavior that we now consider to be codependent. He said, "When we lose a near and dear friend, upon whom we have set our hearts, it should be a caution unto us not to set our affections too firmly upon others. . . . Our affections should be placed upon God and His work, more intensely than upon our fellow beings." (*Teachings of the Prophet Joseph Smith* [TPJS] p. 216.)

EXAMPLES OF CODEPENDENCY

Examples of codependency include the mother who needs her children to do well in school, go on a mission or succeed in sports so she, the mother, looks good. It is the housewife who cleans her house until she almost destroys her physical health so that others will think she is a good housekeeper. It is the man who follows the same pattern of overwork in his employment. It is the woman who needs her boss to like her so much that she forms an inappropriate relationship with him.

Codependency waters down any service relationship. A codependent teacher teaches in a way that makes her students suffer by equating her own self-worth with the performance of her students. In attempting to fill her own extreme needs, she pushes the students to achieve without regard to their growth. In a similar way, a codependent leader attempts to fill his own needs and causes those he serves to suffer.

A codependent mother responds inappropriately to her children because she needs their approval, and the children suffer as a consequence. Such a parent may have a difficult time setting limits and following through on consequences. For example, Jim and Sue told their twelve-year-old son that he could not be out after 11:30 at night. Sue needed her son's approval so much she could not discipline him, and her son knew it. When he came in late, she accepted his excuses even though she felt they were inappropriate. This created a conflict between her and her husband who wanted to have his son suffer an appropriate consequence: not going out the next weekend. This son had never heard of the words "codependent" or "enabling," but he knew his mom would get him out of whatever he wanted her to. By enabling him, she was keeping him from assuming responsibility for his own behavior.

A codependent tendency is evident in the leader who can't lead because she is paralyzed by over-concern about what others think of her. It is also evident in the nurse who is so involved in and upset by the suffering of her patients that she must resign.

Codependency is the young person who steals or shoplifts because of peer pressure. It is manifest in the actions of a young girl who allows a young man to take advantage of her even though she has been taught and believes the gospel teaching of moral cleanliness.

Codependency is the wife who allows her husband to continually abuse her and then believes him when he tells her it is all her fault; it is the member who marries one messed up person after another so she can "fix" them. Codependency is the mother who, when her son makes a serious mistake, becomes sick, even hospitalized, from the stress. It is the primary teacher who goes inactive when she fails to fulfill her own expectation to be a perfect teacher, or at least succeed with each of her students. It is the leader who is so frustrated with the mistakes of others that he resents his coworkers and is unable to maintain good working relationships.

Codependent people are the ones who enable or rescue other people from the consequences of their behavior. (Imagine what it would be like if the Lord did that for us?) Joseph Smith taught the opposite of codependency when he said, "I teach people correct principles and they govern themselves." (*Journal of Discourses*, 10:57-58.) The gospel does not teach us to be codependent. Our own upbringing and/or member teachings do.

As we continue our journey out of bondage, we learn to more clearly identify codependent behaviors. For more information on the difference between what the gospel teaches and codependency distortions, see page 80 in *The New Stress Reduction for Mormons*, Chapter Eleven.

How Can I Tell if I am a Lot or a Little Codependent? How Can I Tell if Healing is Taking Place?

One sister asked, "How do I know whether I'm a little bit or quite a bit codependent? Is all of this called codependency? Please help me understand where I am, as well as identify my progress."

As with this sister, many struggle to understand different types or stages of codependency, how codependent service is different from gospel service, and how selfishness is part of codependency. To help answer these questions, the codependency continuum was developed.

Selfish (A) ———▶ Codependent ———▶ (B) Christlike

Comparing Various Levels of Codependency to the Degrees of Glory

In Doctrine and Covenants 88:29, the Lord said, "Ye who are quickened by a portion of the celestial glory shall then receive of the same, even a fulness." President Marion G. Romney taught that if we add the word "now" as follows, we would understand this scripture's application in our own lives: "Ye who are quickened [now] by a portion of the celestial glory shall then receive of the same, even a fulness."

The scripture continues, "And they who are quickenend [*now*] by a portion of the terrestrial glory shall then receive of the same, even a fulness. And also they who are quickened [*now*] by a portion of the telestial glory shall then receive of the same, even a fulness."

In a similar sense we can be quickened *now* by a desire for understanding of or an awareness of our codependency tendencies. This will help us experience healing of our codependency. Let's consider how the concepts of degrees of glory may be applied to the new codependency continuum.

Telestial (A) ⟶	Telestial/Terrestrial ⟶	(B) Celestial
Selfish	Codependent	Christlike
Thinks only of self	Provides service with strings attached	Provides service with the pure love of Christ

As shown on this codependency continuum, codependency is somewhere between complete selfishness and Christlike service. As we consider this application, we can conclude that perhaps, for many, codependency is a step in the right direction, a step toward gospel service. Is it not better to be codependent than to be interested only in self? The problem is that codependents tend to give service with negative strings attached—service motivated by selfishness, control, fear, anxiety, hurt, etc. The codependency continuum illustrates our ultimate goal of charity: the ability to provide Christlike service with unconditional love.

Codependency is better understood when one considers where the person is on the codependency continuum.

When people are wondering whether or not they are codependent, the questions often asked are: "How do I find and define the line between being codependent and not being codependent? How can I know if I am codependent?"

Rather than asking a black and white question "Am I codependent?" they could ask, "In what direction am I moving?" To answer this question, consider the section of the continuum between "totally selfish" (point A) and "gospel service" (point B.) Codependency is found somewhere between being totally selfish and being able to give gospel service in a Christlike way.

However, on this continuum, a person may be a very selfish codependent (just above point A) or have very little selfishness (just below point B), yet this whole area is still codependency.

Consider the following description of the needs of a codependent person at point A, and another at point B. Notice how vastly different each description is, even though both are codependent.

Point A

- Her needs are overwhelming to the point of consuming the relationship. She will do almost anything to maintain a relationship, even if she is abused.
- She will do what he needs, even if she breaks commandments she believes in keeping.

Point B

- Her needs are still very important, yet she is almost in control. Her needs now dilute her service very little. She is learning to serve others because of a desire to help, support, guide, and save souls with love.
- She is learning to shift her allegiance to the Lord rather than to any other person. She is learning to follow Christ and to follow others who follow Christ.

Within this continuum, there are many levels of growth. There is a great difference between telestial and terrestrial codependency, and celestial Christlike service. To better understand these stages, consider the writings of a recovering codependent who progressed through each of these stages from selfishness to Christlike service.

1. Telestial Codependency: Overwhelming Needs/No Awareness/ Total Denial/No Responsibility for Self.

My needs almost control me. They dictate what I will do in my relationship with you. My only awareness is how to please you. I am miserable if I do not please you, and for an unknown reason, I am also miserable when I do. My consuming desire is to please you in whatever way necessary. Nothing works for me, and I don't know why.

(She is unhappy and miserable, and has so much denial, she has no idea what is causing her problem.)

2. Lower Terrestrial: Strong Needs/Developing Awareness/Decreasing Denial/Increasing Self Awareness/Responsibility Turns to Self-blame.

My needs strongly influence me, but I am now able to recognize how strong they are. I am gaining some awareness of how much of a problem codependency is for me. I have difficulty controlling my needs, but I am now aware that they exist. My guilt sometimes leads me back into denial, but I now sense that there is a better way to live. I don't understand it, but my reduction in need and developing awareness motivate me out of denial to experience some spiritual growth. I'm not sure I even know the questions, must less the answers, but I feel a difference inside of me. I now realize I am responsible for my own behaviors and mistakes, but knowing of that responsibility leads me to beat myself up so much I then feel guilty and depressed.

(She is learning to be responsible for herself, but she is turning that new awareness into self-blame with statements such as: "Oh great! Now I have learned about another thing that I do wrong, another on my long list of mistakes I have made. Now on top of the list of my weaknesses, I must add codependency." This attitude hurts her progress, and so the adversary will feed this attitude as much as she will allow him to.)

3. Middle Terrestrial: Strong Awareness Which Is Replacing Denial/Balanced Needs/Increased Personal Responsibility/Developing Emotional and Spiritual Growth.

I am now aware of how sick I was when I was willing to do almost anything to gain the approval of another person. It has been hard for me to recognize, but I now understand my own selfishness in that process.

I understand that when I verbalized my motive for serving others, both the verbalization and the service were a means of meeting my own consuming need for approval from others. I still struggle with finding a balance between my own needs and giving service in a Christlike way that meets the needs of others (gospel service), but the whole process is beginning to become more clear to me now.

(Although it has been difficult for her, she is beginning to understand how her own needs and selfishness contributed to her codependent behaviors. She no longer says: "How can my motives be selfish? I'm just trying to help people.")

I have a new insight that is most interesting: the fine line between codependency and selfishness on the codependency continuum (point A) was only unclear when I lacked awareness of the truth about myself. Once the Lord helped me move beyond this line, it became more clearly defined.

I have learned that if a person has to ask where the line is, the very question tells something about where they are in understanding their own codependency. As they progress beyond the line, they will clearly see where the line was, as did I.

I am beginning to like myself in spite of the fact that I have weaknesses.

(She is now learning to take her newly discovered awareness and turn it into responsibility for herself, instead of turning it into self-blame.)

4. Upper Terrestrial: Growth from Continually Developing Awareness/Much More Responsible for Self/Developing Love for Self, Others, and the Lord.

I have discovered another fine line, but this line is between codependency and Christlike service. This line becomes more clear as I develop more love for myself, for the Lord, and for others. I now feel and receive the healing love that comes from myself, from some others, and always from the Lord. This healing love is changing my life. As a result of this love, my self-esteem is increasing by leaps and bounds. I can't believe I was ever so unaware, and I no longer need to continually beat myself up for it. I'm just thankful that the Lord is blessing me.

I can no longer excuse my sins. In becoming more aware of sins I need to repent of, I find my desire to repent and become clean before the Lord has also increased. It is similar to the experience of the Nephites who heard about the atoning blood of Christ from King Benjamin: "And they had viewed themselves in their own carnal state, even less than the dust of the earth. and they all cried aloud with one voice, saying: O have mercy, And apply the atoning blood of Christ that we may receive forgiveness of our sins, and our hearts may be purified; for we believe in Jesus Christ, the Son of God." (Mosiah 4:2.)

Her Desire to Become Clean Increases

I want to rid myself of all my sins so I can be clean before the Lord, and I want to stay clean. The Lord said, "For I the Lord cannot look upon sin with the least degree of allowance." (D&C 1:31.) I do not want to minimize or rationalize any of my sins. I now find myself repenting of old sins more deeply, as well as present behaviors I never felt were wrong before (such as when I treat others inappropriately).

She Is Beginning to Recognize the Difference between a Weakness and a Sin

While my greatest desire is to become clean before the Lord, I am also discovering within my heart the difference between sins and weaknesses. In my search of the scriptures to help me understand this, I find the following conclusions very comforting.

My Sins: I want to repent of all my sins and I understand better that a sin must not be minimized, rationalized, or denied. It must be repented of because "no unclean thing can enter into his kingdom; therefore nothing entereth into his rest save it be those who have washed their garments in my blood, because of their faith, and the repentance of all their sins, and their faithfulness unto the end. Now this is the commandment: Repent, all ye ends of the earth, and come unto me and be baptized in my name, that ye may be sanctified by the reception of the Holy Ghost, that ye may stand spotless before me at the last day." (3 Nephi 27:19-20.)

My Weaknesses: My weaknesses are different. It is more difficult to repent of a weakness, for unless I am thinking inappropriate thoughts and acting upon them, they do not become sins. My weaknesses of the flesh can lead to sin if I act upon them. For example, my weakness for food does not become a sin unless I eat too much, etc. A weakness for pornography can remain only a weakness and not become a sin unless one thinks inappropriate thoughts or seeks out and views pornography. I should not feel guilty because of a weakness, but I do need to be careful and humble about my weaknesses. They can become sins far too easily. I have found that when I repent of my sins, they are gone and I have peace. For me, it is not the same with my weaknesses.

I have found no scripture in which the Lord commands me to repent of a weakness, but I have found scriptures to comfort me that he would help strengthen my weaknesses. I love the words of the Prophet Ether:"Fools mock, but they shall mourn; and my grace is sufficient for the meek, that they shall take no advantage of your weakness; And if men come unto me I will show unto them their weakness. I give unto men weakness that they may be humble; and my grace is sufficient for all men that humble themselves before me; for if they humble themselves before me, and have faith in me, then will I make weak things become strong unto them." (Ether 12:26-27.)

She Is Developing Increased Patience

I am becoming more patient with myself, yet I still can't excuse my weaknesses the way I used to with words such as: "That's just the way I am"; or "You think I have problems. Let's talk about you"; or other things I have said such as, "I've always been like this, and I'm too old to change now." I read a quote by Elder Marvin J. Ashton in the Church News *(16 September 1989) that summarized my exact feelings: "That's just the way I am" will not be used as a crutch or excuse for lack of progress, but rather we will use God's gifts and the example and strengths of others to live better today and hold on to principles that are eternal."*

She Is Developing Love for Self and Others

I can now love myself even with my weaknesses because I am building upon the foundation of the gospel of Jesus Christ. This has become very important to me, for healing cannot occur without the foundation of faith in the Lord Jesus Christ, repentance of all my sins, and having the Holy Spirit with me.

She Is Developing Humility and New Awareness of Her Own Issues

I have prayed for humility and meekness before the Lord, and for the blessings that he knows I need, not just the blessings I seek from him. This process has helped me deal with one of my codependent issues as I sought for humility. As I developed more humility and meekness, I feared that I would become weak and would allow others to take advantage of me again. This fear was displaced as my understanding grew. Humility and meekness have become some of the greatest strengths I could have in my life. The Savior refers to himself as "meek and lowly in heart." (Matthew 11:29.) Alma instructed his son Helaman to "Teach them . . . to be meek and lowly in heart; for such shall find rest to their souls." (Alma 37:34.) I have come to recognize pride as an advertisement of an abundance of weaknesses and possibly even sins."

I better understand the following scriptures, which continually strengthen me in my quest for humility and peace: "And inasmuch as they sinned they might be chastened, that they might repent; And inasmuch as they were humble they might be made strong, and blessed from on high, and receive knowledge from time to time." (D&C 1:27-28.) "Be thou humble; and the Lord thy God shall lead thee by the hand, and give thee answer to thy prayers." (D&C 112:10.)

Her Need to Impress Others Is Decreasing

Because of these truths, I am becoming more kind to myself. I more easily give myself credit for the progress I have made, and I continually thank the Lord for his help, which makes my progress possible. Rather than being consumed with guilt, I am filled with thankfulness and love. I am more willing to admit my mistakes, and I feel less need to appear "all together" to others. I no longer feel that if my weaknesses are seen, others may not like me. I am now able to like myself as I make progress toward overcoming my weaknesses. It feels good to let down this big defense.

Her Tolerance for Weaknesses in Leaders Is Increasing

There is another aspect of weaknesses which is both comforting and inspiring to me. I have come to realize that leaders in the Church can often be men and women who are living lives of purity and righteousness, yet who still have weaknesses. Sometimes these are major weaknesses, which decrease their ability to serve the Lord. I am much less judgmental of the behaviors of my leaders who show their weaknesses (such as not listening to others as well as they might, or not responding as patiently as they might with a clerk at the airport). Such weaknesses no longer bother me. I now see many good men and women, called by the Lord to serve others, in spite of their weaknesses. And doesn't that apply to all of us who have any calling in the Lord's Church? I remember J. Golden Kimball's statement about leaders: "Some are called to lead us, and some are called to try us." I can now laugh with him, rather than agree with his statement with disdain.

The Healing Power of Love Is Becoming More Real to Her

I now realize that to feel love, I need to develop love for the Lord, for others, and for myself as well as feel love from myself, from others, and from the Lord. As I grow spiritually and emotionally and the healing of my codependency progresses, I start to recognize love from other people. I now feel the love from the Lord that was there all the time. I realize it was my own issues that kept me from receiving this healing love. I was too busy beating myself and feeling guilty. As I feel the Lord's love, I become more able to love people, and I can now give love in an entirely different way than when I was trapped in my selfish codependency. For the first time in my life, I understand how the Lord can command us to love ourselves. It used to seem so inappropriate to me.

My main goal is to become a more Christlike person and to have Christlike love, as the scripture in Moroni 7 says. That scripture counsels me to pray with all the energy of my heart to have this love that he gives to those who are "true followers of his Son, Jesus Christ." (Moroni 7:48.)

It used to be difficult to give love when I didn't experience it. Christlike love is unconditional love, and requires us to develop the ability to separate the person from the behavior. I can now love others even when they make mistakes, because I can love the person, and dislike the behavior—yet I do not allow anyone to mistreat or abuse me. The stronger my commitment to righteousness, the more accepting I become of others and their frailties.

Her Faith in Christ and in Herself Is Increasing

In the past I thought I should only have faith in Christ and not in myself. The result was that my own self-esteem decreased. This was very confusing to me until a stake president taught me to have faith in both myself and Christ. He never knew how clarifying that was for me.

She Is Learning to Make Fewer Excuses

This is not an excuse system, it is an acceptance system. It is important to understand the difference. I don't excuse my mistakes, but I love myself the way I am because the Lord does too; now I can love others the same way. The adversary wants us to use an excuse system. He may suggest, "Oh, you didn't really make a mistake. And if you did, it wasn't really your fault anyway, so why should you feel guilty?" Or he says, "You're so bad that it doesn't really matter anyway. You've made so many mistakes and got things so messed up that it doesn't really matter now." Both of these lines of reasoning keep us in denial and in codependency.

She Is Learning to Choose Her Pain

I've come a long way from my life of denial which caused a lot of pain, hurt, and need for repenting. I really didn't want to go through the pain of this healing process, but it has been worth it. David Holindrake said, "Choose your pain." When we are talking about progress, there is pain when you stay where you are, and pain when you move ahead. You choose which one you really want. I wouldn't want to go through it again, but I'm thankful for the experience. As someone said, "The truth will make you free, but it might first make you miserable."

She Is Learning that Everyone Has Issues Which Can Be Clarified

As I continue to face new issues I never knew were a part of my life, I have come to realize that we all have issues. The problem is that many of these issues are denied, or ignored, or used to justify weaknesses and even sins. As I sought to understand and receive more humility from the Lord, I came to realize I had to face my own issues and my misunderstanding about humility.

I have learned that the more we repent of our sins, the more we free ourselves to more clearly understand and deal with other issues that we did not recognize before. To try to deal with issues without first spiritually cleaning the slate is similar to eating on dirty dishes and stating that the dirty plate has no effect on the food we place upon it today.

As I have sought help from a professional, I discovered things about myself which I did not like, such as my tendency to blame others and to victimize instead of being responsible for my own behaviors. For instance, when I felt pain, fear, or rejection, I immediately shifted to a personal issue of mine that until that time, I never knew was a part of me. I concluded that I did not need to listen to my counselor and that I could feel justified in my hostility toward him because he was teaching me "psychology," not the gospel.

As I clarified this new issue with myself and the Lord, I came to realize that the Lord also wanted me to look honestly at myself, to quit denying my pattern of blaming others, and quit giving my own free agency away to others through victimizing. Incredibly, I also came to realize that the hostility I dumped on my counselor reflected the very pattern I used with others, especially family members, whenever I felt threatened or was under stress. When I admitted this, I began modifying my own patterns.

She Is Learning that Even When She Is on the Right Track, Growth Takes Time

I also realized that even when I am on the right track, it takes time to grow. Joseph Smith said, "When you climb up a ladder, you must begin at the bottom, and ascend step by step, until you arrive at the top; and so it is with the principles of the gospel— you must begin with the first, and go on until you learn all the principles of exaltation." (TPJS, p. 348.)

She Is Learning to Be Responsible for Her Own Happiness

I am also learning to be responsible for my own happiness. If someone contributes to my happiness, that is nice. If they don't, I am still responsible for my own happiness. I consider this truth in terms of 2 Nephi 2 to learn to "act" rather than to be acted upon.

WHAT DID SHE DO, AND HOW DID SHE DO IT?

This sister has now developed a strong, gospel-based awareness which has replaced her denial. Her needs have become more balanced, and she has accepted increased personal responsibility. She is developing some real emotional and spiritual growth, and some stability in her life.

At the upper level of terrestrial service on the codependency continuum, she is feeling and receiving healing love from the Lord, and it is changing her life. She used to be the type of person who, when she made a mistake, would beat herself up and conclude that the Lord couldn't love her. When asked about her experience, she said, "It is almost as if the codependency and pain are draining out as I allow and feel the healing love from the Lord." She has almost reached celestial service because of healing her codependency.

THE JOURNEY OUT OF THE BONDAGE OF CODEPENDENCY

For many, recovery from codependency is a lifelong journey; for others, it takes years. But for all, it is a journey from wherever they are on the codependency continuum to celestial service. Since almost anyone may be codependent to some degree, then perhaps we all need to make this journey at some time. Many of those in service occupations (and many parents) must make this journey out of the bondage of codependency in order to effectively serve others.

There are examples from the scriptures of people who were in bondage at some time. For instance, life was hard for the people of Anti-Nephi, and their leader, Zeniff, whose over-zealousness led him to be deceived by the Lamanite king and to be in bondage to the Lamanites. As they learned to trust in the Lord, they were delivered from their bondage, and life became easier. (Mosiah 7.)

Alma and his followers departed into the wilderness and escaped when the Lord warned them of the coming of King Noah's army. (Mosiah 23:30-31.) Later, Alma and his people were discovered and persecuted. The persecution became so intense that they pleaded with the Lord to deliver them from bondage, but deliverance did not come quickly. Instead, the Lamanites placed more difficult burdens upon their backs and life again became more difficult. This people responded by drawing closer to the Lord and the Lord made their burdens light. The Lord heard their prayers and delivered them in a miraculous manner.

Codependency is a bondage to any person who needs approval and needs to help or control others too much. We can learn how to apply gospel principles, as did Zeniff and Alma, and journey along the continuum out of the bondage of codependency.

CONCLUSION

I would suggest that you not read this book all at once. Rather, take time to ponder and pray about each chapter and its possible applications in your life to help you increase your relationship with the Lord. Give yourself time to learn, grow, heal, and receive the Lord's love and help. In addition to this book, you may need the help of a

Church leader or professional counselor to do this. The Lord will help you, for as Hugh B. Brown said, "He who made you expects his work to succeed, and will answer a call for help." You are his work. (Moses 1:39.)

 *Chapter 2*

Denial! (Why Do You Believe I Have Codependent Tendencies When I Don't?)

As I Face My Painful Codependency Denial, I Find Hope and Encouragment to Change and Grow

Concerning agency, the Lord said, "All truth is independent in that sphere in which God has placed it, to act for itself, as all intelligence also; otherwise there is no existence." (D&C 93:30.) This free agency is needed for our existence, for our freedom. Yet, through denial, this same agency can be used to decrease our freedom.

Someone has said, free agency is the right to choose what is right, as illustrated in the Lord's words to the Prophet Enoch: "Say unto this people: Choose ye this day, to serve the Lord God who made you." (Moses 6:33.) Free will is the right to choose between right and wrong. Freedom is the result of our choices. Right choices result in increased freedom while wrong choices decrease our freedom. We are in control of what we choose, but not the consequences of our choices. "Abide ye in the liberty wherewith ye are made free; entangle not yourselves in sin, but let your hands be clean, until the Lord comes." (D&C 88:86.)

Codependency is a result of choices which negatively influence the freedom of those involved. As children, we can be influenced to think and believe like codependents and therefore have our freedom limited, both in the present and in the future. As we become adults, we may still relinquish control to other adults, and still not be free. This chapter provides hope that we can experience not only pain but also joy as we face and overcome the codependency we learned in our homes.

Acknowledging this pattern of learned codependency and how our freedoms are still limited can be very difficult, but doing this will enable us to get past our pain to freedom and joy.

Some people use their agency to stay in denial about codependency. This denial makes life harder and also robs them of the joy that can come from true gospel service. Remember, as someone has said, "The truth will make you free, but it might first make you miserable." Yet, as with all truth, after we acknowledge our weakness, our decision to live differently results in increased freedom in our lives.

We all practice denial at times. Although it is certainly prevalent, it is rarely helpful. A famous example of denial occurred in the time of Galileo. In his effort to prove to the priests of his day that the earth was not the center of the universe, he asked them to simply look into his telescope, but they refused. They didn't want to see evidence of anything different from what they already believed.

We are like those priests when we choose denial. We can't overcome a problem unless we admit we have it. The gospel telescope provides us with a look at our need to change—the opposite of denial. It shows clearly that the codependent pattern of denial is fed by fear and selfishness and that it reinforces codependency and prevents healing. It shows that denial builds pride, destroys peace, and prevents us from feeling the pain that can lead to repentance and healing. Perhaps people's general reluctance to "look into the telescope of truth" is one of the reasons President Marion G. Romney said, "The toughest job is to make Latter-day Saints out of Mormons."

WITH CHRIST, WE CAN LEAVE OUR DENIAL AND BE MADE FREE

Only through the Savior can we be made free: "And under this head ye are made free, and there is no other head whereby ye can be made free." (Mosiah 5:8.) If we choose to get out of our denial, we save ourselves pain and misery, both now and later in life.

The Savior may have been speaking about the denial of some Latter-day Saints when he said, "Many will say to me in that day, Lord, Lord, have we not prophesied in thy name? and in thy name have cast out devils? [the Melchizedek Priesthood is needed to do this] and in thy name done many wonderful works? And then will I profess unto them, I never knew you: depart from me, ye that work iniquity." (Matthew 7:22-23.)

MORE EXAMPLES OF THE DESTRUCTIVE INFLUENCE OF DENIAL

Denial creates an inability to recognize a weakness, problem, or sin. Denial is the Church member, who, when confronted with a dishonest act, denies any knowledge of it. It is the woman who marries because she knows that she can "make him into what she wants."

Denial is the Church member who emphasizes the importance of attending meetings, paying tithing, keeping the Word of Wisdom, and even attending the temple while she mistreats and judges others. (This mistreatment may include: yelling at and being impatient with family members, constantly criticizing others, trying to control family members, treating an older child like a younger child, etc.)

Denial is the Church member who passes someone who needs help so he won't miss sacrament meeting or be late for the temple session; or who parks in the handicap spot and does not see anything wrong with it; or who says he doesn't have time to go visiting teaching or home teaching; or who treats someone he does not like as if he were his best friend, then degrades him behind his back.

Denial is the sister who goes to inappropriate movies and justifies it one way or another; or who tells others of the weakness of her non-member neighbors or employees, yet would never admit she is gossiping. It is the employer who criticizes other employees behind their backs or who cheats others during the week, yet sees himself as worthy of a temple recommend.

Denial is the member who wants to know how she should change so her husband will not abuse her anymore. (She has allowed herself to be convinced it is all her fault.) It is the member who keeps choosing friends who lead her into trouble; or the girl who is pregnant with her boyfriend's baby, and although he abuses her and steps out on her, she is sure they will soon be married in the temple.

Denial is the woman who believes that as soon as she finds a good relationship, she will be happy; or, who reads many books on self-improvement as a way to avoid getting in touch with guilt feelings that would lead to repentance and change. It is the person who, in order to avoid honestly looking at her personal issues and need for repentance that were raised in a counseling session, judges anyone who has training in psychology as being out of harmony with gospel teachings.

It is the member who said, "Everything I ever did was for my daughter," when she really did those things so her daughter would perform well so *she* would look good. It is the person who controls others with her illness, whether physical or emotional, real or feigned.

Denial is the man who avoids his own responsibility and failings in his marriage by telling his wife that she is the problem; or the man who tells his wife that her learning about codependency is causing their problems in their relationship and that if she would stick to gospel teachings and not study this psychology bunk, they would be just fine.

Codependency is a subtle selfishness. While the codependent verbalizes caring for another person, there is often an underlying strain of denied selfishness. As we become less codependent and more Christlike, we reduce the amount of selfishness in our lives.

It is important to remember that as a person experiences the healing of codependency and an accompanying reduction of selfishness, it does not mean she should completely ignore personal needs and self-care. Misunderstanding this concept, some codependents have said, "Christ never thought about himself, so I should never think about myself." Perhaps the word "selfishly" should be at the end of that sentence! We can only serve others as we learn to take care of ourselves so we can have the physical, emotional, and spiritual strength to serve the Lord and his children. (For more on this concept, see Chapter One in *The New Stress Reduction for Mormons.*)

A major area of denial for codependents is how they avoid dealing with feelings. They often attempt to medicate negative feelings so they do not feel them. A common approach for LDS codependents is to keep so busy that they successfully avoid getting in touch with negative feelings. The challenge develops when they are too tired to avoid feelings by keeping busy. They must either face their feelings or shift to a different pattern, one that requires less energy. They often choose to eat too much food, watch inappropriate movies, or mesmerize themselves with hours of television.

THE CODEPENDENT STAGES FROM DENIAL TO RECOVERY AND HEALING

There are stages we can go through in life such as:

1. Total Denial
2. Some Awareness of Denial
3. Decreasing Denial
4. Increased Awareness
5. Emotional and Spiritual Growth
6. Love from and to Self and Others

Although we can stay at the first stage all of our lives, the gospel of Jesus Christ teaches us to be honest with ourselves and avoid denial. Someone said, "The tensions, and they are sometimes traumatic, between our struggle for God and our struggle for truth are due to our ignorance of both."

Missionaries help many out of spiritual denial as they learn the truth about the gospel and join the Lord's Church.

As we increase in honesty with self, we also increase our awareness and gain new spiritual insights. We need a path that goes from denial, to awareness, to growth and then to the healing power of love. It may not be an easy trip, but the struggle can lead to great joy.

FAMILY DENIAL

Families also experience denial as a unit. A family in denial is one where members are sure they can work together to fix their alcoholic dad or their hypochondriac mom, for example. Denial is the mother who waters the marijuana plants belonging to her son because she does not realize what they are; or who ignores the symptoms of drug abuse and feels she doesn't need to know them because her children "would never have a drug problem."

When one family member is having a problem, it is not uncommon for the entire family to become emotionally, physically, and even spiritually ill. They may say, "Well, Dad doesn't really have a problem, " when he is abusing his own children; or, "if we keep it a secret, then it will not become a real problem." They may say of the person who is abusing others, "They do not have a serious problem. They are just struggling as we all do."

Many who struggle make life more difficult because they deny the reason they have the problem at all. For example, denial is the woman who can't lose weight because if she loses it, she risks feeling that people might not like the real her. If she retains her weight, she can continue to say, "they just don't like me because I'm fat."

HELPING OTHERS BE MORE RESPONSIBLE BY "ROBBING" (COUNTERING) COPOUTS

We all use copouts. A copout is any attempt to put the responsibility for our own behavior on somebody else. People who are more mature use fewer copouts. Immature people, on the other hand, always have someone or something to blame for their own problems and behaviors.

Larry has many copouts. His counselor reflects on Larry's one and only counseling session:

> I remember Larry well—a very immature man in his late twenties who came in for counseling. He was the type of person who always blamed others for his own behaviors. I was surprised that he came at all because such people rarely feel a need for counseling for themselves. Larry said, "I'm here because I have come to realize that I have a lot of problems."
>
> I responded by saying, "That is an important insight, Larry. As we realize we have problems, we can then make progress in overcoming them." It was here that Larry said, in total seriousness:
>
> "Yes, I do have a lot of problems, but I have come to realize that they are all the result of living with a wife who has many problems. I now realize that if I can get her to do better, my problems will be solved."
>
> Then I realized that the real Larry was still there—he hadn't changed at all. He still believed that his problems were caused by someone else. In this case, he felt it was his own wife that needed to change, not him. I never saw him again.

Codependents, in their zeal to "fix" others are very susceptible to this attitude. It is important that we remember that our responsibility is to change ourselves—not others. The only righteous dominion we can exercise is over ourselves. Copouts keep us from doing this.

TYPES OF COPOUTS

We will identify four types of copouts. They are "If only," "Things will get better when," "Because, " and "As soon as."

If Only:
- My parents had raised me better.
- I had more money.

- We had a better bishop.
- I had a better job.
- I had a different boss.

Things Will Be Better When:
- We get a new house.
- Bill retires.
- I lose twenty pounds.
- I get married.
- I am no longer codependent.

As soon as:
- The kids are raised, I will relax.
- I finish this degree, I will take time for my children.
- Susan changes, I will be fine. (Says Bill)
- Bill changes, I will be fine. (Says Susan)

Because:
- My mom was a poor mother, I'm a poor mother.
- I came from a dysfunctional home, I'm the way I am.
- I was abused as a child, I'm the way I am.
- Of the way you are, I am the way I am.

Each of these copouts is an attempt to divorce ourselves from our own responsibility. With a "because" copout, we are saying, "I'm this way because of you. It is your fault I am the way I am." In actuality, though, we don't have to stay the way we are regardless of what made us that way. We can change our self-chosen attitudes that prevent us from growing and experiencing the joy of progress.

For example, Tony lives in a place where it rains a lot, and is humid. Tony hates humid, wet weather. He constantly complains about it saying, "If only the weather were better, I would be a happier, more effective person." Tony is living a copout, for he is saying he can't be happy because of the weather. His problem is about to be solved, for Tony has just learned that he has been transferred to a place where the weather is everything he wants it to be.

Tony has now arrived at his new destination where all of the problems he has blamed on the weather will now disappear. He will be a better person because the weather is what he wants it to be. Let's listen in on a conversation as he steps off the plane.

"Tony, how do you like the weather here?"

"It is so hot! I never dreamed it would be so hot here. I certainly hope it isn't this way all the time. And it is dry—more dry than anywhere I have ever been."

Tony will always be unhappy as long as he does not want to change his attitudes. Until he is ready to accept responsibility for his own behavior, the weather or something or someone else will always be seen as the cause of the problems in his life. When he accepts responsibility for his own behavior, the weather will cease to be a problem in his life. Accepting responsibility is a major breakthrough in a codependent's road to recovery and joyful living.

This does not mean that as soon as Tony matures, he will wake up the next morning and love wet, or hot, dry weather, but rather that he will no longer blame the weather for his unhappiness or ineffectiveness.

Alice and Rick have been married for only a year. They have both been married before and are especially desirous to have this marriage work out. They love each other sincerely, but are unhappy. Instead of communicating, they have become adept at manipulating each other. Rick constantly manipulates Alice with angry outbursts and refusals to talk. She manipulates him by threatening a divorce which she does not really want.

Alice blames Rick for her failings and also for the problems in their marriage. In an attempt to help her become aware and stop using this copout, their counselor used the skills of letting reality be the judge and keeping responsibility properly placed to help her discover, and then nullify, her copout. She spoke with Alice while Rick listened:

"Do you feel everything will be all right in this marriage as soon as Rick changes?"

"Yes, I do," was the strong answer.

"Let's say that he doesn't change and that the divorce you are threatening comes about. Can we assume that?"

"Yes, especially today we can assume that."

"If that does happen, do you think you would ever date again?"

"Yes, I would for sure. I am still a young woman."

"Let's assume then that you are now divorced, you are a free woman again, and you are now dating. Do you think you would ever get serious with someone again?"

"I think I would. If I could find someone better, I think I could have a happy marriage."

"Let's assume that you date and meet someone who is exactly what you have always wanted. He is so wonderful that you can hardly believe it. He is nothing like Rick. (Rick was getting worried about where this conversation was going.) *You decide to get married to this wonderful guy, and you are happy about your plans. Can you imagine that?"*

"Yes, I can." (From Rick's perspective, she was becoming a little too excited about what she was imagining.)

"You have been married now for just over a year, and then one terrible day you discover the horrible truth. You realize this marriage has all the same problems as your present marriage. What will you do then?"

She responded very flippantly, *"I would divorce him."*

"Then, when will it ever end?" was the next question.

Alice was no longer flippant, but became very pensive and thoughtful. She thought for a long time without saying a word. When she finally spoke, she said with much emotion, *"I guess it never will end, will it!"*

"If that is true, what are you going to do about it?"

"I guess I better solve the problems we have in this marriage. I really do love Rick and I know he loves me."

Robbing Alice's copout or denial of her responsibility for the problems in her marriage was very helpful to her because she loved Rick and wanted to stay married to him even though she blamed him for her problems. When she was willing to be responsible for her own behaviors, she was able to work out her problems in their marriage.

In the beginning of this conversation, Alice didn't want to accept responsibility for her behavior. By letting reality be the judge and placing responsibility back on her, where it belonged, she was able to accept and change both herself and her commitment to her desired marriage.

We can also learn to help others be more responsible so that they can enjoy life more fully and relate to others in healthier ways. (The skills mentioned early in this counseling session: "letting reality be the judge" and "keeping responsibility properly placed" will be discussed in greater detail in Chapter 4.)

BUT WHAT IF MY COPOUT IS REAL?

Judy's copout was that she couldn't be a good wife because Josh was a poor husband—he drank and he was constantly losing jobs due to continual arguments with employers. When asked about her copout of blaming Josh, Judy's comment was:

"But it isn't a copout for me to say that I would be a good wife if he were a good husband. He really is a lousy husband and father. My copout is real!"

Many copouts are based on real problems, and the reality is they can make life very difficult. Judy is right not to expect herself to walk around unconcerned and happy about her problems. She can also recognize that while she can be in control of her own life, she cannot control Josh. Since she is the only person she can control, she can begin to take responsibility for her own behavior and be as happy as she can under the circumstances. When she gets up in the morning, she doesn't need to say to herself, "Now, isn't it wonderful that I have a rotten husband, who is home again today to argue with me instead of working to pay all the overdue bills."

What she can learn to say is, "While I'm not happy with my husband being home today or with our home situation,

I can learn to cope in a healthy way by thinking healthy thoughts even though things are not as I wish they were today."

She can learn to think thoughts such as, "I can be happier if I focus on my own responsibilities and if I don't allow him to blame me for his problems, " instead of, "I'm going to be miserable as long as he is unhappy, unemployed, and not paying the bills."

As she learns to take responsibility for herself, her healthy thoughts set her up to cope in a more healthy, productive way under her still difficult circumstances. Unhealthy thoughts set her up for unhappiness that was increased by her attitudes about her difficult circumstances.

HEALING OUR SPIRITUAL DENIAL LEADS TO HEALING OUR CODEPENDENCY DENIAL

Sincerely repenting of sins and becoming clean before the Lord will bring peace. Too often we fight the very process that brings this peace. As incredible as it may seem, a good member of the Church can use scriptures and gospel teachings to justify remaining in denial. Jason, for example, was so afraid of job hunting after losing his job that he stayed home to avoid the pain of possible rejection. He justified his decision by verbalizing that he had faith that the Lord would take care of him and his family because he had always paid his tithing. Later, when he realized his denial and the financial and emotional pain his denial had caused his family, Jason said with deep regret, "My problem was, I did not understand nor apply the scripture, 'Faith without works is dead.' (James 2:26.) My attitude was, 'I have faith the Lord will make it work out, ' even though I was not willing to do my part. My wife repeatedly counseled me to find a job, but I didn't listen."

When asked how he finally got out of denial, Jason said, "Nothing could get me out of my denial until my financial world caved in, for reality had to break through my denial.

Now that life is better, I still seek the Lord's help on a daily basis because without him I cannot succeed. However, I now ask, 'Help me to do my part so I don't make more foolish mistakes that hurt me and my family.'"

Codependents who serve in a manipulating way can remain in denial, clinging to the belief that they are "serving others" as the gospel teaches. In the meantime, they neither provide Christlike service nor grow in the gospel. Their spouses, friends, or even Church leaders, may have no success in helping them out of denial because they are convinced they are following the gospel teaching to serve others. The codependent is often a very good person who may require a life crisis (financial, physical, emotional, or spiritual) before he clearly sees his codependent tendencies.

Many an LDS codependent is pursuing a path they feel is true gospel service while surrounded by people they feel don't understand them. If they did understand, they would never mention this psychology thing called "codependency." *The irony is, the gospel does not teach us in any way to be codependent.* Quite the opposite. We have to learn it from other sources. The gospel teaches the kind of service and healthy self-esteem which heals codependency.

Once we understand denial and recognize that it is causing us problems, we are ready to improve our ability to deal with feelings.

 *Chapter 3*

Why Do I Have Trouble Dealing with Feelings? How Can I Learn to Deal with Feelings Better?

Have you ever been taught that you came from a dysfunctional home, and because of this, you never learned to deal effectively with feelings? That is only part of the story.

In dysfunctional families we also fail to learn how to meet our own needs in healthy ways. Unwritten, unspoken rules tell us: "don't talk" about problems, "don't feel" feelings, and "don't trust." (Black, Claudia. *It Will Never Happen to Me.*) Someone else has suggested that these rules also include: please others, be strong, hurry up, and be perfect.

To those who have been taught that their dysfunctional family experience is a permanently crippling part of their lives, *this chapter provides hope for recovery, healing and an opportunity to learn ways to deal with feelings!*

I witnessed this healing in the family of a close friend who was weighed down with concern for her children. The model home she so desperately wanted to provide them was, in reality, very dysfunctional because of the personal problems of both parents. In spite of her efforts to love them, teach them the gospel, and provide a good home, she was going through a very difficult divorce and felt that her husband had become a very negative influence on the children. Because she felt much guilt and responsibility for messing up their lives, she sought a blessing, and with the inspiration of the Lord, was told that her life difficulties would actually become a blessing that would make the children stronger and more capable in facing their own life challenges. The inspired message came as a surprise to both of us. At the time, I did not understand that we could totally recover from our dysfunctional families. This message brought her relief and comfort, as it can bring comfort to each of us.

The estimated 70 percent of us who grew up in dysfunctional homes can become functional, healthy adults, and so can our children! For an article in *Psychology Today*, Steven and Sybil Solin were interviewed in regard to their new book, *Resilience: How Survivors of Troubled Families Keep the Past in Its Place*. They said that more children grow up and leave sick homes as healthy adults than we thought, for "if you have an alcoholic parent, the risk that you're going to be an alcoholic is around 15 percent. In other words, 85 percent are not alcoholic . . . 90 percent of the children of schizophrenics don't become schizophrenic"; and "The extent to which child abuse is transmitted over generations is six times normal—30 percent become abusers: 70 percent do not." ("How to Survive (Practically) Anything." *Psychology Today*, Jan./Feb. 1992, pp. 36-39.)

MY OWN DYSFUNCTIONAL HOME

Both of my parents were raised in dysfunctional homes. My dad's father was an alcoholic, his mom died when he was young, and his relationship with his stepmother led him to leave home and join the rodeo. My mom was raised by a mother with many health problems, who rarely left her home, and her father was absent both physically and emotionally. Because of this, I was also raised in a dysfunctional home, where my inactive parents never taught me the gospel. Thankfully, great men who served as my Aaronic Priesthood quorum leaders had a profound influence upon me. I have forgotten their names, but not their influence, because their love touched my heart. I knew that their concern for me was more than just a calling for them.

When I was fifteen years old, I read a book entitled *Mormon Doctrine Plain and Simple or Leaves from the Tree of*

Life written by Elder Chas. W. Penrose (1888.) As I read about the first principles of the gospel and the restoration, a testimony of the gospel sank deep into my heart, and the atonement of the Savior became a most important part of my life. My dysfunctional home issues (which I wish I had understood then) led me to overreact and beat myself up unmercifully because of my sins and mistakes. What I felt in my heart, though, was real. My life was changed, and my healing had begun. It needed to, for gaining a strong testimony of the gospel did not eliminate all my other problems.

OTHER LABELS COMMONLY USED

In addition to the term "dysfunctional," labels such as COA ("Child of an Alcoholic") or ACOA ("Adult Child of an Alcoholic") are also commonly used when the subject of codependency comes up. These titles are not limited to children of alcoholics, for anyone from a dysfunctional home can have the characteristics of a COA or ACOA. These characteristics include the tendency to be afraid of authority, to be intimidated by anger, to seek approval of others, to be either overly responsible or irresponsible, to judge self and others too harshly, or to confuse love with pity. The lack of training in dealing with feelings, especially one's own, is a fundamental problem in the life of a codependent. It means a person can identify the feelings of twenty people in a room, yet not his own.

Do codependent people and ACOA's have these tendencies all the time? Not necessarily, but when under stress, negative tendencies tend to surface. If we understand this, we can prepare ourselves to make the proper adjustments when we experience increased stress.

If we were criticized a lot as a child, for example, under stress, our tendency is to be overly critical. If we can understand this, we can prepare ourselves by seeking the Lord's help to avoid being critical when under stress. As one father said, "I wish I had understood this principle sooner. Now that I understand, my preparation and prayers help me control this tendency to be critical under stress, and I respond more appropriately to my children. I no longer blame my children, my wife, or my boss for my weaknesses."

STAGES OF RECOVERY FOR A PERSON RAISED IN A DYSFUNCTIONAL FAMILY

My own experience of recovery and my ongoing healing from my dysfunctional home has led me to recognize what I believe are four stages of healing. These stages are as follows:

1. Denial

At this stage, I had no awareness that my family had problems. As I look back, I recognize that I went through two stages of denial: The first denial came from a lack of understanding that I could benefit by acknowledging and understanding my family's problems.

In my next stage of denial, I acknowledged the problems but responded: "All families have problems, and my family's problems were not unusual." Later, I realized that I avoided awareness of the seriousness of the problems in order to avoid feeling my codependent need to fix them.

2. Awareness/Blaming

At this stage, I turned my awareness of my family's problems into blaming and anger. When I became fully aware that I had a lot of problems as a result of being raised in my dysfunctional family, I blamed my parents, with anger, for my problems. This anger led to some decisions that hindered me and to some which benefitted me. I detached myself from my family and developed strong goals to succeed in the academic world. When I moved to Ohio to work on my doctorate, this detachment helped me so I never felt homesick.

Still, I remember being upset, even with the Lord, for sending me to a family with so many problems. I wished for a family that was active in the Church like some of my friends had. I tried to "fix" my family by attempting to initiate family home evenings. I preached to my poor parents continually. I felt responsible to fix everything (a common ACOA issue).

In my own mind, I became a victim. It was at this stage when, as a sophomore at Weber State University, my studies increased my awareness of my own personal and family problems. I became more angry as the weeks passed. As I walked across campus one day, the Lord clearly told me in my mind that I did have problems as a result of my family, but I was now eighteen and responsible for myself. If I accepted this responsibility for myself and quit blaming others, I could overcome these problems.

3. Acceptance/Growth

I did not understand at that time the depth and importance of the Lord's counsel, but, fortunately, I followed it. On that day I started to overcome my problems. This teaching enabled me to recognize and accept the influences my family had on me, without blaming. I learned what Paul Mayer meant when he said, "Blaming our faults on our nature does not change the nature of our faults." This acceptance enabled me to overcome and grow emotionally and spiritually. Positive, active acceptance leads to growth. On the other hand, passive acceptance often leads to victimization without hope. For the first time in my life, I realized I could become a healthy, Christlike person in spite of my problems!

The Lord's counsel, plus my strong testimony and faith in gospel teachings, saved me from a life of anger, blaming, and even depression. Now, as I look back, I wish I had sought counseling immediately to help me work through my own issues more quickly and in more depth. Even so, life became enjoyable for me as I worked toward my goals and because of my desire to help others.

4. Gratitude

I did not realize the stage of gratitude for past problems and challenges existed until many years later, when I came to realize the blessings that my dysfunctional family had brought into my life. This stage provided healing of many negative feelings. I came to realize that, had I not been raised in such a totally dysfunctional family, I would not have learned what I have learned and would not be able to help others with their struggles. This may be true for many people.

I also came to realize that we can be in stages three (Acceptance/Growth) and four (Gratitude) simultaneously and happily remain in them for the rest of our lives.

The deciding factor is whether we turn toward or away from the Lord when we have serious problems. My response to my dysfunctional home was to seek the Lord's help to heal me, and that has made all the difference. While it has been a painful struggle, and still is at times, there has been much real joy in the struggle.

How to Identify a Feeling

We must first gain an awareness of our feelings before we can identify them. Someone has said that if we can put "I think" in place of "I feel," then what we are considering is not a feeling, but an idea. For instance, if we say, "I feel you are too task oriented with the children," this is an idea, because we could also say, "I think you are too task oriented with the children." If we say, "I feel sad, " this is a feeling because we wouldn't say, "I think sad."

After a feeling has been properly identified, what do you do if it is a negative feeling? There are four steps that can help you let go of negative feelings:

1. Gain awareness of what you are feeling.

2. Practice this so that the next time you feel this feeling, you become aware of it more quickly. As this skill develops, you can more easily recognize various feelings.

3. Respond by feeling the hurt and acknowledging or validating the pain. Once a negative feeling is validated you will be able to let go of it.

4. Give yourself time to learn this skill. It takes time and practice.

When you feel a negative feeling and don't stuff it, but feel it, become aware of it, validate it, and acknowledge it is there, you can then let go of the negative feeling permanently. A validated negative feeling can be purposely released and when it is gone, it promotes a healing within.

For some, it may be necessary to have help from a church leader or a professional counselor to learn to deal with feelings, and that's okay. This process takes time, especially for those who have never learned how to validate negative feelings. Elizabeth Kubler-Ross must have understood this when she said, "Somehow we think it's not all right to feel bad. The next book I write is going to be called, 'I'm Not OK and You're Not OK, and That's OK.'"

Her insights led to the identification of stages of mourning—denial, anger, bargaining, depression, and then acceptance—that people go through when they learn that they have a terminal illness. (Charles G .Morris, *Psychology—An Introduction*, Seventh Edition, Prentice Hall, p. 400.) When we experience a negative event, such as learning of a terminal illness, it is not uncommon to first feel denial that it is really happening, then anger, followed by bargaining with God to prevent death, then depression that such a negative event has happened, followed by acceptance that this is our lot in life. The same stages seem to apply with many of life's challenges. Understanding these stages can help us deal with the negative feelings we may have with other types of difficult experiences such as divorce, trauma, or loss of any kind.

DEFINING ANXIETY, HURT, ANGER, GUILT AND DEPRESSION

David Viscot, in his book, *The Viscot Method* (Houghton Mifflin Co. Boston, 1984, p. 54), provides the following definitions that can be helpful in understanding our feelings. He defines anxiety as "future hurt, or the expectation of hurt or a loss." Hurt is "present pain, or the experience of loss *OR* of injury." Guilt is "past pain, unexpressed or anger held in and turned against yourself." (See Chapter Nine of *The New Stress Reduction for Mormons*.) Depression is "past pain—chronically unexpressed. It is the pattern of reacting to all hurt by holding in the anger." These definitions can be very helpful because they describe a "feeling cycle" that begins when we expect to be injured, so we become *anxious*; we are saddened by our loss, so we feel *hurt*; we resent being hurt, so we are *angry*; but containing our anger hurts us, so we feel *guilty*; but our guilt depletes us, so now we are *depressed*. (*The Viscot Method* Houghton Mifflin Co., Boston, 1984, pp. 53-54.)

UNDERSTANDING INSECURITY, GAINING AWARENESS, AND DEVELOPING SKILLS

We all feel insecure at times. As codependents, we often perceive that all the *sources* of our insecurities are outside ourselves. With this belief, it is easy to assume that the *solution* is also outside ourselves. We seek to fix or control others in order to change our insecure feelings. We can do this with little or no awareness of what our motives really are.

The first step to overcoming insecurity is to recognize that it comes from within ourselves. When we learn to change our perception that our insecurities are caused by other people and seek inner healing from the Lord, only then can we increase our own feelings of security.

STUFFING AS AN INAPPROPRIATE WAY TO AVOID DEALING WITH NEGATIVE FEELINGS

Elizabeth is very much in love with Neal. She wants to marry him, but he recently told her that he would like to always be friends, like a brother and sister. She felt that she dealt with this very difficult situation extremely well, for she did not become angry; she did not cry or express any negative feelings.

However, soon after this experience, Elizabeth went home to visit her parents. They were thrilled to see her and invited her to stay for dinner. She was poised and happy and showed no signs of her negative experience with Neal until her mom suggested that if she would study harder in school, her grades would be better. Elizabeth blew up at her mom, accusing her of never understanding her. Her outburst was so strong and violent that her parents withdrew, afraid to say anything else.

Mom and Dad have just become the victims of Liz's stuffing. Her hurt, anger, and even rage, in this case, had been carefully and unknowingly stuffed inside, with no awareness that these feelings had been stuffed. She was like a volcano ready to explode, waiting for any situation that might touch on the hurt and release all the anger.

GUILT OR SHAME AS WAYS OF DEALING WITH NEGATIVE FEELINGS

John Bradshaw said, "Guilt is when we feel like we have *made* a mistake, but shame is when we feel we *are* a mistake." Shame is difficult to get rid of and is a very common feeling of those who are struggling with addictions, whether it be addiction to alcohol, drugs, food, sex, or people. Dave Featherstone said, "No one can deal with shame alone. There is only one cure for shame, and that is knowing that God loves you and that you are of infinite importance to him." He is totally right.

BLAMING AND JUDGING AS WAYS TO AVOID DEALING WITH NEGATIVE FEELINGS

When we feel pain, hurt, or guilt, it's easy to blame or judge others. We might target parents, spouses, children, employers, or anyone else for our failings, problems, or even sins. This does not work. Joseph Smith taught, "We are full of selfishness; the devil flatters us that we are very righteous, when we are feeding on the faults of others." (TPJS, p. 241.)

We all experience pain and hurt in our lives. The Savior experienced more than all of us. We can know the gospel is true, repent of our sins, and still have the weakness of blaming others, or finding and focusing on the faults of others. When we blame or judge others, it shows a weakness from within ourselves because—

- How we feel about ourselves is how we tell others they are.
- We criticize others when we feel hurt.
- We judge others when we feel hurt, guilty, or troubled.
- We judge others by behavior and ourselves by intent.
- We feel jealousy because of our own feeling of inferiority.
- We find fault as a way to justify our decision not to get close to others, to avoid being hurt. We then blame them for our inability to be close to them.

Richard L. Evans, in "The Spoken Word" radio broadcast on 21 April 1968, spoke of these concepts as he quoted Dr. Neal A. Maxwell who said, "If I am not happy with me, other people suffer." Elder Evans continued, "Our attitude and actions toward others often depends more upon how *we* feel than upon what *they* do. When we are tired or troubled we may react impatiently, severely; but when we are relaxed and untroubled, we may react quite differently to precisely the same situation. What we feel inside, what we know concerning ourselves, often determines our reaction to others."

What a difference this insight could make in our spiritual growth and our healing, for Elder Evans continued by saying, "On the other hand, we tend to dislike those whom we have wronged and mistreated because we dislike ourselves for doing it—and when we dislike ourselves, we dislike others also. . . . It is bad enough to suffer for our own mistakes, but worse to make others suffer for things they didn't do. The remedy is to live in honor and morality and cleanliness and kindness, keeping the commandments, meeting responsibilities so we can avoid accusing ourselves and quarreling with conscience."

Joseph Smith said, "The little foxes spoil the vines—little evils do the most injury to the Church. If you have evil feelings, and speak of them to one another, it has a tendency to do mischief." (TPJS, p. 258.)

Elder Marvin J. Ashton, in the April, 1992 General Conference, called this process "bashing." "None of us are yet perfect, " he said, and "Through microscopic examination, one can find in almost every life incidents or traits that can be destructive when they are magnified. . . If the adversary can influence us to . . . bash and undermine, judge or humiliate, half the battle is won. It neutralizes us spiritually. The Spirit of the Lord cannot dwell where there is . . . any kind of bashing. . . . None of us needs one more person pointing out where we have faltered or failed . . . Whatever happened, " he said, "to giving others the benefit of the doubt?"

The gospel teaches us to not judge others. "Judge not that ye be not judged. For with what judgment ye judge, ye shall be judged; and with what measure ye mete, it shall be measured to you again. And why beholdest thou the mote that is in thy brother's eye, but considerest not the beam that is in thine own eye? Or how wilt thou say to thy brother, Let me pull out the mote out of thine eye; and, behold, a beam is in thine own eye? Thou hypocrite, first cast out the beam out of thine own eye; and then shalt thou see clearly to cast out the mote out of thy brother's eye." (Matthew 7:1-5.)

Neal A. Maxwell summarized it well when he said, "The more serious the work on our own imperfections, the less we are judgmental of the imperfections in others." (*Not My Will, But Thine*, p. 95.) The Prophet Joseph Smith said, "If you do not accuse each other, God will not accuse you. If you have no accuser you will enter heaven, and if you will follow the revelations and instructions which God gives you through me, I will take you into heaven as my back load. If you will not accuse me, I will not accuse you. If you will throw a cloak of charity over my sins, I will cover yours—for charity covereth a multitude of sins." (TPJS, p. 193.)

VICTIMIZING AS A RESPONSE TO NEGATIVE FEELINGS

Victimizing is when a person says, "The way I feel is determined by you, for you make me the way I am." There are often three steps to victimizing: (1) "You make me unhappy, but (2) as soon as you change, then I will be happy; however, (3) if you don't change, then I will remain unhappy, and it will be all your fault." Some victims complain all the time in a way which someone has called "rehearsed anger."

Notice at each step we give an increasing amount of our free agency to another person. A victim is a martyr who responds as if he or she is the "poor me" person who can't be happy because someone else has "made" him or her unhappy. (It is important to know that these concepts do not directly apply to a person who is being abused. The solution in an abuse case is to stop the abuse and then, as part of the process of recovery and healing, work on overcoming the tendency to victimize.)

All children victimize at times, but some children form a victimizing attitude which sometimes makes them even more difficult to help than rebellious kids. No matter what you do for them, it's never good enough. They always seem to find a way to feel bad. We can select a group of five children (one of whom is a victim), take all five to a movie, and buy each their favorite treat. Four of them will be happy but the victimizer will come home feeling bad. The more you try, the more ground you seem to lose with a victimizer.

How can we stop our own victimizing? We begin by catching ourselves feeling sorry for ourselves, and then ask, "Why do I feel a need to feel sorry for myself?" If we are honest with ourselves (without denial), we often find we actually enjoy feeling sorry for ourselves or having others feel sorry for us!

It helps us to avoid victimizing if we do not personalize what others say or do. It is good to be sensitive—but not too sensitive—to the feelings of others. When we personalize what others say, it is easy to victimize. Victimizing can also set a person up to commit many sins, including the sin of adultery. In this instance, the victim is led to the rationalization that "because everyone else does not understand me, it is okay to form a relationship with someone who does understand me."

BUT HOW CAN I HANDLE NEGATIVE PAST EXPERIENCES SUCH AS ABUSE OR A RAPE WITHOUT VICTIMIZING?

Many have had negative experiences such as abuse (either as a child or as an adult), rape, loss of a loved one (in a dating or marriage relationship), the entanglements of divorce, difficulties of being a single parent, addiction of any kind (to people, food, drugs, sex, or television), accidents, health problems, etc. The feelings from these experiences can make life very difficult, especially if we overly blame others or circumstances for our feelings.

It is never easy to find the line between accepting and working through valid negative feelings. It can also be hard to find the right time to develop the ability to let go of these feelings and move on in life. Some well-meaning people do us a great disservice by telling us, "Well, just quit feeling that way." This insensitivity makes it difficult to process feelings, get them behind us and move on in life. Working through the issues can take time, and the time line is different for each person.

Church leaders can be very helpful if they understand the struggle an abused person can go through and help them process the feelings appropriately. However, they can contribute to the abuse if they do not understand the abused person and simply negate these very real and legitimate feelings.

Abuse is especially difficult if the victim is young because children view themselves as the center of their world. When a person does a bad thing to a child, often the child feels it is his or her fault, and so he or she must be bad. The opposite can also happen. For example, one girl was raised in a healthy family. However, when still quite young, she was abused. Her early positive experiences enabled her to separate herself from the experience and not conclude that she was a bad person because of it.

Others have great difficulty separating the experience, so instead, they separate themselves from it by disowning their feelings. In so doing, their emotions often become negative. Some abused children become very negative, pessimistic people. With the help of a counselor, many get reconnected with their emotions. (See Chapter Thirteen in *The New Stress Reduction for Mormons.*)

WORK YOUR OWN PROGRAM

When I worked with patients in drug programs, we taught them, "Work your own program, not someone else's program. You can't work your own and another person's program at the same time." We often focus on another person's faults to avoid dealing with our own, and it works. It enables us to avoid the inevitable pain of personal growth. In fact, it can work so well that we rarely focus on our own negative feelings. However, that whole process prevents us from changing or repenting.

TASK ORIENTATION AS AN INAPPROPRIATE WAY TO AVOID DEALING WITH NEGATIVE FEELINGS

Many codependents use "busyness" to successfully avoid negative feelings. While this task orientation is a problem, a more serious problem can develop if burn out occurs. The person must either face their feelings or shift to a different pattern, one that requires less energy. They may choose to eat too much food, watch inappropriate movies, mesmerize themselves with hours of television, or even indulge in pornography or sexual sins.

As codependents, most of us are vulnerable to such patterns to some degree. The Lord can help us break these patterns. As Jim, a recovering codependent, said, "I now understand why the Spirit continually prompted me to spend more time in the evenings in prayer and reading the scriptures. After being "too busy" all day to have to face my feelings, my tendency was to avoid painful feelings in my relationship with my wife by watching television into all hours of the night. This easily led to watching inappropriate movies on television until guilt had destroyed my spirituality. Only repentance helped me recognize my pattern and break it. How much easier it would have been for me to follow the original prompting which would have prevented my negative pattern from developing."

Many codependents become too "task oriented" in their struggle to understand the difference between being "task" and "people" oriented. They have learned how to be successful by setting and achieving task-oriented goals, often to the detriment of person-oriented goals.

When we have too much to do, it is easy to focus on accomplishing goals to the degree that we neglect relationships. We can, for example, focus so much on getting the children to bed on time that we fail to see how we hurt our relationship with our children (not to mention their self-esteem) by the methods we choose. Yet we may see yelling and spanking as appropriate because the children are not going to bed (thus preventing the accomplishment of our important task). Other examples include criticizing a member of the family in front of others because he did not do what you asked, insensitivity or even verbal abuse to an employee who is not helping enough with an important task, or publicly humiliating an employee who is not performing well enough to help the manager reach her task-oriented goals.

We need to pray for the Lord's help to get in touch with true feelings and to avoid task orientation. But codependents tend to pray *fast*. We may pray quickly so we can get on with the next task. We are so used to focusing on tangible things to accomplish, that we may see prayer as "nonproductive" time. When we pray, we need to be careful not to let our minds focus on the many things we need to get done.

As a recovering codependent, I have found myself getting up in the middle of a prayer and running off to do something with no awareness of how I ended the prayer. I have found it healing to ask myself, "What feeling did I have while I was praying that encouraged me to avoid it by moving on to a task?" The answer to this question can provide very revealing answers to the motivation of our task orientation! Prayer invites the very honest examination of feelings, and task oriented people often use tasks to avoid having to examine their feelings. Consequently, we short-circuit the very prayer process that can be a key to our recovery.

We need to pray, and we also need to listen. A helpful prayer analogy is picking up the phone and dialing our Heavenly Father. Often when he answers, we hang up and run off to complete an important task. The Lord is willing to listen to us speak and to answer back, but before he has a chance to reply, we are already gone. We wouldn't do this to a friend we called on the phone, yet our task orientation causes us to do this with the Lord. As we control task orientation by praying, listening, and feeling the Lord's love for us, we experience healing.

Working parents may be guilty of another type of task orientation because they come home after a work day of being rewarded for being task oriented. When they come into the house, they attempt to help everybody get things in order. They say, "Why don't you have this room cleaned? I told you to clean it two days ago. Why are you watching television instead of doing your homework?" They go over their lists of tasks, thinking they are being very helpful; instead they may only be avoiding operating at a feeling level.

LIVE IN THE PRESENT, NOT THE PAST OR THE FUTURE

One way codependents avoid dealing with feelings is to try to live in the past or in the future. The gospel teaches us to live in the present. "Sufficient unto the day is the evil thereof." (Matthew 6:34.) Concerning the past, we are to repent, leave it behind us, and move on. There is no way to accomplish this except through complete repentance.

Concerning our future, we are to live so we can have faith and hope as we look ahead, and use time to plan for a happy future.

Robert Louis Stevenson said, "Anyone can do his work, however hard, for one day. Anyone can live sweetly, patiently, lovingly, purely till the sun goes down. And this is all that life really means." "Happy the man and happy he alone, he who can call today his own; he who's secure within can say, 'Tomorrow do thy worst for I have lived today.'" (Horace.)

In spite of this guidance, "The irony of life is that we're either anticipating happiness or reflecting upon it." We either live in the past or we live in the future, but Psalm 118:24 teaches us that, "This is the day which the LORD hath made; we will rejoice and be glad in it."

Hugh B. Brown said, "Speak to God first thing each morning, then through the day remember that you're going to talk to him again that night."

A major way we make life complex is by trying to live in the past, the future, and the present all at the same time, and we just can't do that. "Live each day that it will always be, when tomorrow comes, a happy memory."

The question is, how can we live effectively in the present? One answer is to realize how we get ourselves into what someone has called our "dead past" by doing "if onlys" to ourselves. "If only I hadn't married Jim, if only I hadn't made that mistake, if only I had not committed that sin, if only I had been more patient, if only I hadn't had that child, if only I had not become codependent," and the list can be endless. We can learn from the past, but we can't change it and don't need to stay in it.

"If onlys" and past mistakes tend to get us stuck in the past. We all make mistakes. I have made more mistakes in my life than I ever thought I would. Some of these mistakes have made life more difficult for myself and my family. The adversary wants us to dwell on our mistakes. Babe Ruth hit 714 home runs, but few people know that he had

1,336 strike-outs. We don't remember him for the strike-outs, and neither should we remember ourselves for our strike-outs. We can repent, learn from them, and focus on the things we did right.

It helps us understand the importance of leaving our past when we consider the feelings that "if onlys" create. Whenever we do an "if only" to ourselves, we create guilt, despair, depression, hopelessness—all negative feelings—and these negative feelings get us stuck in the past. Although the gospel of Jesus Christ teaches us to repent so we can put our past behind us, codependents too easily continue to beat themselves up, even after the Lord has forgiven them. We get stuck in our "dead past" because we've stuffed so many negative feelings for so long, that when they come to the surface and we feel them, they almost overwhelm us. One result: we get stuck back with our negative feelings. As mentioned earlier, a sin *can* be repented of and put behind us. A weakness *cannot* be repented of unless it becomes a sin, and with the Lord's help, it can even become a strength.

We may also prevent healing if we try to live in the future. Someone has said we do this with a lot of "what if's" to ourselves. "What if I can't fix him? What if my daughter gets pregnant? What if I make a mistake? What if he doesn't like me? What if she doesn't like me?" Or, "what if we have a car accident?" Some people go through more terror and turmoil worrying about whether they will have a car accident or other tragedy than if they actually had one.

Our "what ifs" create negative feelings, such as fear and anxiety. We can fill our lives with so much fear and anxiety that we can't even function. If we live in the present with the realization that every life has negatives come into it, we are more prepared when they come. Negatives are a part of life. We came down here knowing that we would be surrounded by potential accidents, diseases and germs, and that people could hurt us; yet we came willingly and "shouted for joy." (Job 38:7.) If we expect that negatives are going to happen and quit worrying about that possibility, it helps us to stay in the present.

We worry without realizing that worrying is a habit. Worrying is something we do because we don't know how to deal with feelings very well. Elder LeGrand Richards, at age ninety-three, was asked his secret of a long, happy life and he quoted his favorite poem, "To every worry under the sun, there is a remedy or there is none. If there be one, hurry and find it; if there be none, then never mind it." (*Ensign* Nov. 1991, p. 14.)

What feelings do we have when we live in the present? We can more easily feel peace, calmness and joy, for as Collette said, "What a wonderful life I've had. I only wish I had realized it sooner." Someone else said, "Don't worry about the future. The present is all thou hast. The future will soon be present, and the present will soon be the past."

 *Chapter 4*

How to Overcome Codependency-Related Communication Problems

Ronald had a growing testimony of the gospel and was the only member of the family who was active in the Church. He had married an LDS girl in the temple, but the marriage was on rocky ground. He was contemplating divorce and was in great turmoil when he came to see me. I spent an hour explaining to him that if he were living the principles of the gospel completely he would not be having these problems. I explained why he should change and how wonderful life would be if he did. My intention was to help Ron, and I was convinced that I had; after all, at the time, I felt I had taught him truth, and that was what he needed.

Ron got his divorce and became inactive in the Church. I felt bad that he had not seriously considered what I had taught him—I knew that could have prevented his tragedy. Many years later, I learned that I failed to help Ron not because I lacked the desire to help him, but because I didn't know how to communicate with him in an effective way. I have since learned that preaching (I now realize that's what I did) actually hurt his spiritual growth. I realize that there *are* communication skills that can allow us to help others.

If we want to be able to bless the lives of others, we first have a responsibility to become as healthy and as Christlike as we can. When I worked as a counselor in a drug-treatment program, parents would often say, "We love our daughter so much we would do anything to help her! What is the best thing we can do?" My answer: "Become emotionally and spiritually healthy yourselves. The more healthy you become, the more you can help her."

The more healthy and less codependent we become, the less we need others to fulfill our needs and the more we are able to communicate with others in Christlike ways. Some people think that communicating with others in Christlike ways means that we will always be kind and loving and have no conflict in our lives, but that is not the case.

Common weaknesses in a codependent's life are (1) difficulty in communicating with others, (2) failure to recognize manipulation by self and of self (3) difficulty recognizing feelings, and (4) lack of skills to deal with conflict in healthy ways. This chapter is written to provide strength to overcome these weaknesses so we can learn to communicate better with others, to avoid manipulation, and to deal with conflict more effectively.

A SCRIPTURE-BASED COMMUNICATION MODEL

In Matthew 28:19-20, the Savior gave these instructions to his apostles, "Go ye therefore, and *teach* all nations, baptizing them in the name of the Father, and of the Son, and of the Holy Ghost, *teaching* them to observe all things whatsoever I have commanded you."

There is a significant difference in meaning between these two early Greek words that are both translated into English as "teach." In fact, this scripture forms the basis for a communication model that, when applied, can help us help others in more effective ways. The first of these words that mean "teach," explained in footnote 19a, means "preach to, make disciples of" (meaning make Christians of). The second of these, also translated "teach" in English, has a much different meaning than the first. As footnote 20a says, the other meaning for teach is "post-baptismal teaching."

Missionaries are called to preach to people and call them to repentance, but after these investigators join the Church, then go to a Sunday School, seminary, or institute class, we should not preach to them, but instruct them. There is a difference between preaching to people and instructing them. Confusing these ideas and preaching when we should be instructing, as I did unknowingly with Ron, can limit our ability to communicate and help others.

As we learn how to apply the scripture in Matthew (quoted above) to communicate with others in more Christlike ways, we are more able to help them grow emotionally and spiritually. The basic model was originally developed by C. Kay Allen, in Denver Colorado, and is used with permission.)

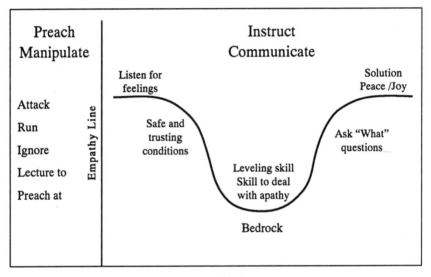

This model can help us identify ways that we manipulate others, and it can help us learn to communicate in more Christlike ways. Since manipulation is a fundamental symptom of codependency, it is important to learn how to avoid it. Let's consider various sections of this model so we can learn to communicate rather than manipulate.

Why We Manipulate and How to Recognize When We Do

When we display the characteristics shown on the left side of the model above, we may manipulate by attacking, running away from, or ignoring another person. We may manipulate with anger or apathy, or preach to or blame others for our own behaviors. We try to solve communication problems by lecturing and preaching, trying to control in subtle or not-so-subtle ways, or by telling others what they should do. We may not be aware that this is what we are doing, and we may justify our preachy approach with gospel teachings (as I did with my friend, Ron).

We all practice manipulation to some degree. Parents often manipulate because they believe they *should*. They believe that they are at fault if their children make mistakes and so they try to control children to prevent them from making mistakes. Others manipulate because they need to "be right" at all costs. Being task-oriented rather than person-oriented also causes codependents to be more manipulative (as discussed in Chapter Three.)

The scriptures teach us to influence but to absolutely avoid control or manipulation. In the revelation on the priesthood, the Lord said: "We have learned by sad experience that it is the nature and disposition of almost all men, as soon as they get a little authority, as they suppose, they will immediately begin to exercise unrighteous dominion." (D&C 121:39.) People can exercise this authority in their roles as parents or teachers or in relationships and church callings.

We all have the tendency to respond to people using the characteristics found on the left side of the model, but we can learn to do better. This same revelation continues: "When we undertake to cover our sins, or to gratify our pride, our vain ambition, or to exercise control or dominion or compulsion upon the souls of the children of men, in any degree of unrighteousness, behold, the heavens withdraw themselves; the Spirit of the Lord is grieved; and when it is withdrawn, Amen to the priesthood or the authority of that man." (D&C 121:37.)

This strong doctrine cautions all of us (not just priest-hood holders) to avoid responding to others in controlling ways. We can learn to respond using righteous communi-cation, for "no power or influence can or ought to be main-tained by virtue of the priesthood, only by persuasion, by long-suffering, by gentleness and meekness, and by love unfeigned; By kindness, and pure knowledge, which shall greatly enlarge the soul without hypocrisy, and without guile." (D&C 121:41-42.)

These scriptures teach us to communicate in very spe-cific, Christlike ways. They also teach us better ways to deal with conflict. Let's consider the model on page 54 as an approach that can help us apply these scriptures.

THE EMPATHY LINE

So that we become helpful to others, rather than manipu-late them, we need to first consider the Empathy Line. (Look again at the model on page 54.) This line suggests that before we can help anyone, we must honestly care about them. Unless we sincerely care, instead of learning new ways of communicating and helping others, we will learn new and more subtle ways to manipulate.

THE COMMUNICATION SIDE OF THE MODEL

From the communication side of the model, we learn how to communicate with others in more Christlike ways by first listening to others to understand their feelings. When we *sincerely* listen to others' expressions of their feel-ings because we care, they feel safe with us. We can then reach what is called the "bedrock," or the real problem. After we reach the bedrock, we can continue to help by asking "what" questions in order to encourage the person to find a solution. With these tips in mind, let's consider the parts of this model in detail and how we can apply them.

What Is a Bedrock?

Reaching the bedrock is the purpose of listening to discern others' feelings. Bedrock is the *real reason* people do what they do or say what they say. For instance, in a sacrament meeting where a hundred people are in attendance, each person may have a different bedrock or real reason for being there. People may attend to renew sacred covenants; to gain strength to keep these covenants; to meet friends; to be seen by others; to fulfill their "duty"; or to provide service to others. Codependents may not understand their own bedrocks because they are not in touch with their feelings. It is a liberating experience to discover our own bedrocks.

In order to understand bedrocks better, let's look at Kim, a teenage girl. She once said to her parents," I don't know why you are so narrow-minded when it comes to drugs!" Her statement created a communication problem between Kim and her parents. How can they reach a solution? Most people would try to solve a problem like this by skipping the listening stage and trying to go directly to the "solution." This actually involves preaching and lecturing. The parent might say, "You're taking drugs, aren't you Kim?" or "Why would you say that when we've taught you so well?" Both of these statements are likely to initiate an argument with Kim. Then the parent might give Kim a wonderful lecture—so good it should be printed in the next issue of the *New Era*—as to why she shouldn't take drugs. All the time the parent hasn't listened long enough to learn *why* Kim said what she did.

Behind Kim's statement, "I don't know why you're so narrow-minded when it comes to drugs," there can literally be over a hundred bedrocks: real reasons why she made the statement. This may seem incredible, but it is true. Bedrocks are always the reasons behind a behavior. Some possible bedrocks behind Kim's statement could be: "I'm on drugs"; "I'm seeking help to get off drugs"; "I want to learn how to say 'no' and still have friends"; "My boyfriend told me today that I'm a jerk because I won't try drugs"; "My favorite teacher told me I'm stupid"; "I made a serious mistake and I want to see if I can talk with you"; "I'm feeling guilty and so I want to make you feel guilty," and so on.

Too often, a parent hears a child's words without listening to his feelings or trying to understand them. They assume that they already know what the real problem or bedrock is, and move directly into a lecture.

The real question is, "Does such an approach help the child?" Probably not, because instead of listening to him to discern his feelings to learn the real reason for his behavior, the parent is attempting to manipulate and control with a lecture! As we learn to listen to others express their feelings, we can actually discover what the underlying bedrocks are and increase the probability of helping instead of hindering.

Few teenagers walk up to a parent and say, "Excuse me, but I have a problem, and I was wondering if you would help me." Instead, they say something like, "Why are you so narrow-minded about drugs?" They are hoping the parent will somehow figure out the bedrock behind the statement by listening long enough to understand the real reasons they are saying what they are saying.

HOW TO LISTEN FOR FEELINGS IN ORDER TO REACH BEDROCK

Listening is the foundation of good relationships, and it improves self-esteem. When we listen to our children, we are communicating to them that they are important and worthwhile. When a child interrupts us as we are watching our favorite show with an issue that is very important to him, if we stop and give him our full attention, we are communicating to the child that he is worthwhile.

Whenever we attempt to communicate, we express both words and feelings. Although we often respond only to another person's words, their feelings are actually more important in the communication. If we respond only to someone's words, communication can be a frustrating experience. As we learn to accurately discern the feelings a person is displaying and respond appropriately to these feelings, our ability to communicate improves.

Double Messages

Double messages are common barriers to communication. When our verbal message says one thing and our feelings (or nonverbal messages) say something else, we are communicating contradictory double messages. For example, Cindy and Kevin go on a blind date. Kevin feels love at first sight, but Cindy hopes to never see Kevin again. After the date, Kevin walks Cindy to her door, pauses, looks into her eyes, and his word message is, "Thanks, I had a good time." His feeling message is: "I like you and I want to see you again." Here, the words and feelings agree.

Our codependent Cindy responds, "Thanks, I had a good time, too." Yet her tone of voice conveys her true feeling, "I don't enjoy being with you at all and I hope I never see you again." Cindy's word message is: "Thanks, I had a good time." But her feeling message is: "I don't like you and I don't want to see you again" (or "I like you . . . not!"). The words and feelings disagree, resulting in a double message.

Double messages cause confusion. Congruence is when the verbal and feeling level messages agree. Honesty demands congruency and the open expression of what we truly feel. Codependents prefer to avoid confrontation and conflict. They have a need to please, and they are famous for sending double messages. Such a pattern damages the communication skills of codependents as well as their relationships.

When Cindy sent two messages instead of one, Kevin had to decide which one to believe. The problem is that most of us either fail to hear both messages or we assume that the words express honest feelings. Sometimes we hear both messages, but we respond to the one we *want* to hear. Other times we're not sure which message to believe and we end up confused. When we develop better and more sensitive communication skills, we learn to hear and understand the feelings behind the verbal message.

Confusion can become a way of life for the codependent who denies his true feelings. As in the situation with Cindy and Kevin, if we have negative feelings toward someone who has romantic feelings for us and we try to have romantic feelings when we really don't, we will send a confused message. Losing touch with our feelings is one of the most common symptoms of codependency. Therefore, as we choose to deal with this issue, we foster the healing of our condependency.

LEARNING TO REFLECT FEELINGS

As codependents learn to deal with their own feelings and stop denying them, they can use this new ability to help others in more Christlike ways. Because they are often out of touch with their own bedrocks, codependents may find hearing or understanding the bedrock feelings of others difficult (even though they are very tuned in to the more surface feelings and expectations of others). Be assured that most codependents can *learn* to discern the bedrock feelings of others and reflect those feelings back to those they are talking to. This not only helps others, but helps to heal the codependent.

This process of listening for bedrock is different from the codependent pattern of judging others and trying to change others to meet our expectations. When the codependent learns to listen for bedrocks, he can discern feelings in order to help others discover *their* bedrocks, rather than dealing with his *personal* needs and bedrocks at their expense. The opposite of manipulation to meet personal needs is to listen to others' feelings in order to help them reach *their own* bedrocks and reach *their own* solutions.

Learning to do this leads us to focus on others' needs, not focus on ours. (We focus on our own needs appropriately at other times and fulfill them on a deep spiritual level.) As we learn to hear deep level feelings, we become more able to communicate with others and help them in Christlike ways instead of trying to change them or coerce them into solving their problems according to our methods. Healing codependent patterns of manipulative communication begins with listening.

Listening is the ability to both hear and reflect others' feelings. It means that we are tuned into the feelings of others and then accurately reflect those feelings back to them. This is easier to learn if we pretend to be a mirror that reflects others' feelings, not their words. We listen to their words, but only their feelings are reflected back to them, as shown in the following illustration:

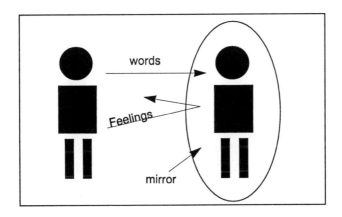

We can learn to hear and reflect feelings using the following steps:

1. Listen for the feeling.

2. Identify the feeling. Summarize it in one word.

3. Mirror the feeling back to the other person.

In step one, we listen fully to the person by tuning into both the words and the feelings that are being communicated. If someone approaches while we are busy, we can stop and give that person full attention. Eye contact is very important to communicate genuine interest.

In the second step, we identify the feelings behind the words spoken. This is often a difficult step for the codependent, but it becomes easier with practice.

In the third step, we mirror or reflect the feelings we have identified by putting into words the feelings we are hearing, and then appropriately sharing them with the other person.

Instead of giving a lecture, Kim's parents could say, "Well, you seem pretty frustrated right now with how we feel about drugs" and then listen!

LISTENING LEADS TO TRUSTING CONDITIONS

People do not generally divulge their real bedrock until they feel safe with us, and they don't feel safe with us until we listen. Listening for feelings leads to safe and trusting conditions. Notice in the following example how a mother sincerely listens to her elementary school child. Consequently, the child feels free to express her real feelings and concerns.

Child: *"I hate school."*

Mother: *"School is hard to stand right now."*

Child: *"It is worse than that. All my teachers hate me, especially Mr. Larson. He makes me feel stupid."*

Mother: *"It bothers you that he makes you feel stupid?"*

Child: *"I hate him! Why should I have to sit by Bill Johnson rather than my friends. He only puts stupid people by Bill."*

Mother: *"You feel being put by Bill is telling all your friends that you are stupid. . . ."* And so on.

This mother is sincerely trying to discern her daughter's feelings. She may not succeed as well as she desires, but her efforts to listen to feelings and bedrocks at least increases her probability of helping her daughter with her real concern.

Had the mother not listened, the conversation might have gone as follows:

Child: *"I hate school."*

Mother: *"What do you mean, you hate school? Everyone in our family always does well in school and likes school. You are smart, and you can do well if you just try harder."*

Child: *"But all my teachers hate me, especially Mr. Larson. He makes me feel stupid.*

Mother: *"What a silly thing to say. First of all, not all of your teachers hate you. I met Mr. Larson at the Parent/Teacher Conferences last month. He was a very nice man who said he thought you were a wonderful and capable student. Now you just listen to what he is telling you so you can get a good grade in his class!"*

In this exchange, the daughter said three words indicating her feelings about school. Instead of listening for more information, the mother assumed from only three words that she knew her daughter's bedrock. She then proceeded to lecture and preach to her daughter.

AFTER BEDROCK, THEN WHAT?

In the example of Kim referred to previously, the parents actually listened with sincerity to understand why she was telling them they were narrow-minded about drugs. They reached the bedrock (her real feelings), which she expressed to them: "I am saying this to you not because I am using drugs, but because I need to know if you will be judgmental of people who use drugs because some of my friends have used drugs."

After any parent has reached the bedrock, the biggest temptation comes: to begin an even better lecture than they would have used before. "You mean you have friends who use drugs? Don't you know how dangerous that can be? They will probably talk you into using drugs too!" If we succumb to the temptation to lecture, we succeed only in teaching our children not to confide in us.

After we reach the bedrock, instead of lecturing, we can effectively help by asking "what" questions. "What" questions motivate others to discover a solution; "Why" questions only bring forth excuses. We might ask: "What do you think we should do? How do you think we can help?" After we ask, we listen again as she shares her solutions. Learning to listen for feelings and ask "what" questions that lead to real solutions takes practice, but the result is worth our time and effort. Children often come up with better solutions themselves than we could provide in ten of our best lectures.

TEACHING SOLUTIONS: KEEP RESPONSIBILITY OR FREE AGENCY PROPERLY PLACED AND LET REALITY BE THE JUDGE

Two crucial concepts in learning to communicate without manipulating are: "Let reality be the judge" and "Keep responsibility or free agency properly placed." These two concepts work together. Developing the skills needed to use these concepts is required in order to avoid using the ineffective lecture approach in our attempts to solve others' problems.

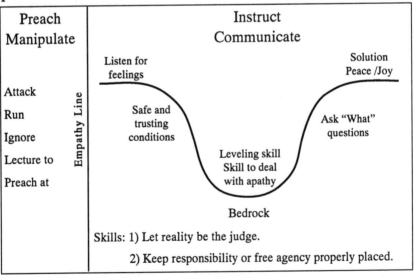

His mother responds: "Bill, when I talked to your teacher she told me you have failed every test, missed class seven times, and failed to hand in four out of five assignments. I can't allow this to continue. If you continue to do this, you will fail this class and possibly not graduate. You don't want that to happen, do you?"

Bill responds by saying, "It's not my fault. Last year Mrs. Jones was a lot better math teacher, and I did okay in her class."

In this example, Mom is *not* letting reality be the judge and she is not keeping responsibility and free agency properly placed. How do we know this? Who is doing most or all of the talking? Mom. Who is taking responsibility for Bill? No, Mom is! Was Mom helping Bill be more responsible? No! Why was she unable to help Bill? (For one, she did not know how to place responsibility on Bill, where it belongs, for not doing well in math.) If Mom accepts Bill's responsibility, she limits his growth and assumes an unnecessary burden.

Let's consider how Mom might have responded more appropriately. If Bill is being irresponsible by not doing his homework, attending class, or taking tests, and if he is also trying to blame his teacher for his behavior, Mom can present him with the opportunity to accept this responsibility. She could say, "How are you doing in your class?" When he says, "Terrible," she could ask, "What will happen if you miss class and don't hand in assignments?" Caution needs to be used so the questions are not asked in a "preachy" way.

Some parents are so overburdened by their codependent habit of accepting their children's misplaced responsibility. that they are frustrated and fatigued, and yet unable to determine the reason for these feelings. One step to get out of this mire is to become aware of who is assuming the responsibility and then learn the skill of appropriately placing it where it belongs.

Understanding the concept of "letting reality be the judge" is important. The opposite of letting *reality be the judge* is to be the judge *ourselves*. When we become the judge, we assume the other person's responsibility. But when we let reality be the judge, the misplaced responsibility automatically falls to the person on whom it belongs.

Consider one of the Lord's dealings with Adam and Eve. The Lord told Adam and Eve not to partake of the forbidden fruit. Eventually, they disobeyed and partook. When the Lord returned, they hid themselves, and he called to them: "Adam, Eve, where art thou?"

At this point, we might ask: "Why would the Lord ask a question to which he knew the answer? He asked in order to help Adam and Eve respond in such a way that they had to take responsibility for their own actions. By asking the question, "Where art thou?" the Lord allowed reality to be the judge and placed the responsibility on Adam and Eve, where it belonged. The Lord could have responded, "Okay, Adam, out of the bushes. I know you are in there. I can't believe what you've done. I left you for only a short time, and you did the very thing you were told not to do." If the Lord had responded this way, he, rather than reality, would have been the judge, and Adam and Eve could have shifted their responsibility onto the Lord. The Lord himself responded in such a way that reality judged Adam rather than God. As we learn to respond in this same way, we will be using Christlike skills to help others.

COMMUNICATION THAT MAKES IT DIFFICULT FOR INACTIVE CODEPENDENTS TO BECOME ACTIVE IN THE CHURCH AGAIN

Some recovering codependent members of the Church remain inactive because of preachy, judgmental, or insensitive communication from active members. These are usually well meaning members who convey messages like the following: "The healing you think you have experienced is bad or phony. It is not the gospel and it is not approved by the leaders of the Church. You have been deceived—especially if you have been going to a non-LDS counselor. No non-LDS counselor can help a member of Church."

These messages can be very disconcerting and confusing when codependents know that the renewal they have experienced has been valid and wonderful and it has healed their feelings. Codependents that receive such messages may lean toward healing their codependency without gospel principles, not because they lack a testimony, but because they have experienced a degree of real healing of their codependency with the help of someone, such as a counselor, outside the Church; and that healing has been discounted by someone in the Church.

Codependents dealing with this issue can benefit by understanding the three levels of healing.

The healing they have experienced has taken place on the "thought" and "feeling" levels of healing and is just as necessary and valid (though not complete) as the next level, "spiritual healing through Christ." This is explained in more detail in Chapter Five, pages 82-84.

(1) Even when they are active in the Church, many codependents attempt to solve their problems on an intellectual, logical, thinking level. This level is an important place to start but is very unsatisfactory in and of itself. Then, as they learn to deal with feelings in more healthy ways, their codependent issues and emotional health greatly improve. They experience a new level of appropriate healing on a deeper, more satisfying feeling level.

(2) When some relief is achieved, some people conclude or are told by others that the Church caused them to be the way they were before. This conclusion leads them to disown their responsibility for former behaviors and to falsely assume that activity in the Church is synonymous with perfectionism, task orientation, and codependency. This inaccurate idea encourages them to stay away from the Church. They do not realize that the gospel of Jesus Christ teaches the opposite of these negative patterns and the Church recognizes that there is a need for healing on the

thought and feeling level. It is only through Christ, however, that we can achieve a more complete healing on the
spiritual level.

(3) Many codependents who find a measure of relief in
inactivity actually fear becoming active again in the
Church. They fear that if they go back to church, they will
go back to their old patterns of being perfectionistic by trying to do too much, and dealing with life in their heads
instead of on a feeling level. They rightfully do not want to
lose what they have gained in learning to deal with feelings—an appropriate and valid stage in the healing
process. This feeling level of healing helps to clarify many
codependent and dysfunctional issues; yet it still falls short
of the top level of spiritual healing through Christ. This
level may remain out of reach as long as the codependent
remains separated from the strength they can find when
they are in full fellowship and activity in the Lord's
Church. Understanding that true gospel teachings will
help the codependent obtain an even deeper healing can
remove the fears mentioned above. Understanding these
concepts can help the codependent heal and can also help
those who seem to believe that terrestrial-level healing is
bad because it is not on the celestial level.

Those who want to help the codependent experience
healing should avoid discrediting appropriate healing
experiences. Rather, they should encourage the codependent to give themselves credit for their progress and at the
same time reach for the next level of healing. Trying to
make someone feel guilty by suggesting that he is bad
because he is only halfway to the celestial level of healing
does not help that person make it the rest of the way.

(4) Codependents are experiencing healing when they
learn to see that their old patterns were indeed *their* own
patterns, and not the Church's. Those patterns were not
caused by activity in the Church, but by misunderstand-

ings, false traditions, and thought distortions. With this understanding, there is no longer a perceived need to avoid the Church. All truth learned in any setting in the past can be retained as the person immerses himself in the additional healing truths of the gospel.

Many negative patterns become a part of our lives because of the way we were brought up or because of the influence of other people. A problem arises when we equate these negatives with the Church or fail to recognize the difference between teachings by members and gospel or church teachings. (See Chapter Eight in *The New Stress Reduction for Mormons*.)

LEARNING TO RECOGNIZE HOW WE DEAL WITH CONFLICT

Is conflict bad? Should it always be avoided? Many codependents would answer "yes" to both questions. Many codependents believe they are not good because they have conflict in their lives. As one sister said, "I am a poor parent and spouse because there is so much conflict in my life. I cannot deal with conflict. If I were a good parent and spouse, I would not be having so much conflict."

Because of her belief that conflict is bad, she has decreased her ability to deal with any conflict, and decreased her self-esteem. Remember, *conflict is inevitable!* Christ experienced a lot of conflict even though he was perfect.

There are healthy and unhealthy ways of dealing with conflict. Some inappropriate ways include attacking someone, running from conflict, and ignoring conflict. These are ways of attempting to manipulate another person and rarely make a conflict situation more bearable.

Attacking Others

We can attack another person using physical, verbal, or indirect approaches. Physical attacks involving bodily confrontation are less common than the verbal or indirect approaches. We will discuss only the latter two approaches.

In a verbal attack, people often resort to exchanging put-downs such as: "I wish you could cook like my mother," and she responds, "I wish you could make dough like my father."

Verbal attacks can escalate into a situation in which each person strives to use a stronger or a more subtle put-down than the other person. Indirect attacks are perhaps the most widely practiced. They are used to attack others in a personally devastating way. More commonly known as "gossip," and masked as concern, these attacks occur when, in our unwillingness to communicate directly, we make angry and damaging remarks about others. Instead of working out our differences, we choose to tear down and ridicule someone else. This causes an increasing amount of damage to our relationships.

If we handle conflicts with others through indirect attacks, we take the risk of destroying trust—the trust we share with the person about whom we are talking negatively, and the trust we have with others as well. When people hear us verbally tearing down someone else, they can appropriately conclude that we will likely do the same to them when they are not around. This can become a serious problem if our perceived "innocent gossip" continues long enough. Not only do we lose the trust of others, but we also may develop a habit of indirectly attacking other people whenever we feel insecure.

Running Away from Conflict

A second way of dealing with conflict is to run away from it. This method involves acknowledging the existence of a conflict and choosing to escape it. We may choose to physically leave, indulge in drugs or alcohol, sleep excessively, become ill, overeat, watch television, or work compulsively.

Any activity can be used to run from a conflict. One bishop said, "I have become aware of how I used to use my church calling as a way of running from conflict with my wife. Whenever we would have a conflict, I would leave and 'do the work of the Lord.' But no matter how right that work was, I was using it as an excuse to avoid having to deal with conflict. Now I choose to deal with and resolve the conflicts I have with my wife. Talking through conflicts and strengthening my marriage improves my ability to do the work of the Lord."

Getting sick can sometimes be a little-questioned way of dealing with conflict. For example, if a student says he is nervous because he is having trouble in a class, he may be told to keep trying. If, instead, he says that his stomach hurts, he'll probably be sent to see the nurse. He learns quickly that he can escape conflicts and problems by feigning or actually developing physical illness.

Ignore Conflict

When we run away, we acknowledge that we have a conflict and then try to escape it. When we ignore it, we deny that we have a problem in the first place, and we may drink and overeat, for example, to escape from the problem. This subtle distinction makes *ignoring* the problem the most dangerous of the inappropriate ways of dealing with conflict. By ignoring conflicts, we compound our codependent tendencies to lose touch with feelings and deny the existence of problems rather than confronting them and solving them.

Some Church members respond to conflict by ignoring it because they believe they should never feel anger. When they do feel anger, they deny it and choose to ignore the situation or person that triggered it. Practicing the "ignore it" method makes Christlike communication with others increasingly difficult. When we are unaware of our own feelings, we can't examine them and share them with others. At inappropriate times and often with undeserving persons, smothered negative feelings are bound to surface, causing added conflict.

Further complications may occur when we use a combination of inappropriate methods for dealing with conflict. Attacking then running, running then ignoring, ignoring then unpredictably attacking are some of the most often used combinations.

Codependents can become masters at using these combinations. The first step to healing is becoming aware if or when we are using these methods.

LEARNING TO USE LEVELING TO DEFUSE ANGER

Because of difficulty in dealing with conflict of any kind, the codependent often responds with inappropriate responses to anger by attacking someone, running from the conflict, or ignoring the conflict. They are frustrated because they realize that listening for feelings and reflecting those feelings back does not work in a conflict situation. For instance, when they are trying to be helpful, many respond to obvious anger by saying, "You're feeling very angry, aren't you?" Simple as it sounds, this practice often backfires; it can be like throwing gasoline on a fire. Other skills are needed.

Let's assume that you have been talking to a neighbor, Sue, about the good qualities of another neighbor, Jill. You have expressed how well Jill takes care of her children and how conscientious she is in protecting them from harm. Unknown to you, Sue has passed your feelings on to her friends in the neighborhood. As it has traveled along the gossip line, your words have been changed from a positive compliment to biting gossip that says that your neighbor's children are difficult, problem children.

You are in your house reading when you notice Jill coming down your driveway in obvious anger. You are about to be very negatively confronted by Jill about what you supposedly said about her children. You could run out the back door, ignore her (you know that would not work), or attack her (you know that would be stupid, and it would scare you too much anyway). You need a skill that will help you deal with what you fear most: conflict.

One way of dealing with anger in a conflict situation is called "leveling." This is a method that enables us to set proper conditions in a tense or angry situation so that healthy communication rather than manipulation can take place. Leveling is a quick, three-step process that become easier with practice.

By learning to apply these three steps, a codependent can gain the skill she needs to communicate with an angry neighbor in a way that diffuses her neighbor's anger. The steps are as follows:

Step One: **Examine your own feelings and verbalize them.**

In step one in leveling, you work first to get in touch with your feelings and to verbalize these feelings. While admittedly, this can be difficult for most codependents, it is a very helpful and important step.

Remember, Jill is coming down your driveway. Instead of running, you go out the door and walk toward her. Even though you are scared, you want to deal with this conflict in a better way than you have previously. When Jill starts to accuse you of saying things about her children that you did not say, you realize why she is mad at you. You examine your own feelings and find that you are feeling very concerned about her misunderstanding, so you say, "Jill, I'm very concerned about what you think I said about your children."

Step Two: **Try to understand and verbalize the other-person's feelings.**

In this step, in addition to understanding your own feelings, you try to understand what the other person is feeling and to verbalize this understanding. You seek to have honest empathy and compassion and to understand why Jill is responding as she is. You combine step one and two by saying, "I'm concerned about what you think I said about your children. You are obviously concerned too."

Step Three: **You set up conditions in which you can deal with the conflict in a healthy way through discussion.**

In this step, you conclude the leveling steps so you can establish conditions in which you can talk with Jill about her conflict with you. The words can be simple. You combine steps one and two and add step three by saying, "I'm concerned about what you think I said about your children. It is obvious' you are concerned too. Can we talk about it?" This simple statement sets up conditions so that a discussion of the conflict can begin and healthy solutions can be explored. In our example, Jill's anger can actually be diffused enough with this approach that she is able to listen and, consequently, the conflict can be resolved.

Two additional tips will help ensure that leveling is successful. First, keep it brief; in fact, be as brief as possible. The more words you use, the less chance there is of setting up conditions needed to solve the problem. There is strength in simplicity when using this method.

Second, keep in mind that the purpose of leveling is to set up conditions that make it possible to discuss the conflict. We do not set up an expectation that we can solve the actual conflict in a few words. Nothing will be solved with these three steps unless the people involved have created an atmosphere in which the conflict can be discussed and resolved.

RECOGNIZING AND AVOIDING HOOKS

A "hook" is an unhealthy pattern of behavior that takes place when we allow the other person's anger to make us become angry and overreact. The more subtle the hook, the more difficult it is to avoid. For example, if a woman says to her husband in an angry voice, "It is all your fault that our son became an addict," it is easy for him to become defensive and get "hooked" and respond, "And you think you have been a perfect mother?"

DEALING WITH APATHY

In addition to the leveling skills we need in order to deal with anger in a healthy way, we also need skills to deal with those who manipulate with apathy. As with anger, apathy can be dealt with by using three important steps that can allow us to communicate with an apathetic person.

Step One: **Identify and confront the person's nonverbal communication.**

When people won't talk with us, we assume they are not communicating. Although this is true verbally, it is not true in terms of nonverbal communication. People communicate nonverbally in very strong ways. We can identify their nonverbal communication by noticing whether they are looking at the floor or ceiling, shrugging their shoulders, or shaking their heads. All of these are nonverbal ways of communication. If we identify one of these behaviors, and confront it, we provide an opportunity for the person to begin talking with us. This can be done by saying, "When you look at the floor, does that mean you don't want to talk about it?" Some apathetic people will start to talk at this point. Others will not, so we go on to step two.

Step Two: **Anxiety-controlled silence.**

At this step, we may repeat what we said in step one, or we can use the leveling skill with a statement such as, "I'm concerned about your performance in school and I think you are, too. Can we talk about it?"

If, after this approach, nothing is said, we simply wait in silence. This is not a "staredown" but rather an anxiety-controlled situation when we allow the anxiety to rise as it normally does in situations in which no words are spoken. In this silence, and while controlling our own nonverbal anxieties, we wait for the increasing anxiety to motivate the other person to talk.

As the other person's anxiety level increases, they may respond with anger because they may be afraid of not being able to manipulate us. We may need to be prepared for a possible negative outburst and to be able to deal with the anger using the leveling method.

Step Three: **Place the responsibility back where it belongs.**

The previous steps will coax many apathetic people into talking, but a few will remain silent regardless of our efforts. We need to be prepared to accept the fact that some people will choose not to talk no matter what we do or say. It helps if we understand that by not talking, they are attempting to place responsibility on us, and that we can help by placing responsibility back where it belongs. We can say, "I feel we are playing a game right now. It's called, 'Let's see if I can get you to talk.' I just want you to know that I am not going to play that game anymore. It is your responsibility to decide when you are willing to talk."

After this statement, even though the other person may not talk, the responsibility is placed back on them where it belongs. Depending on the age of the person and the situation, we might also respond, "If you don't talk, you know the consequences" or "If you don't talk, there are unavoidable consequences such as . . . ." (We *can* sometimes help by providing appropriate consequences in a concerned and nonthreatening way.)

THE NATURE OF SHORT-TERM RELATIONSHIPS

Copendents typically do better in short-term relationships than they do in long-term relationships. Short-term relationships may be easier than other relationships for some codependents simply because they demand so little. It is much more difficult to sustain long-term relationships. Dating relationships may be enjoyable and easy because a person can, for a while, look very good, keep up appearances, and appear to be an outstanding "catch." Yet this same person may lack the skills necessary to have a close, warm, long-term relationship.

A person with the same lack of long-term relationship skills may do well raising young children because they are relatively easy to control, yet be unable to deal with conflicts as the children grow older and become more difficult to control. This same parent will usually view the child as being rebellious, and thus see the child as the problem. But when the situation is better understood, the parent may realize he is only giving a sixteen-year-old child the responsibility and freedom appropriate for a ten-year-old.

In all relationship problems, we need to separate the person from the behavior so we can say, as did the Prophet Joseph Smith, "I love you all; but I hate some of your deeds." (TPJS, p. 361.)

WE INFLUENCE, NOT CAUSE, THE BEHAVIORS OF OUR CHILDREN

Every parent makes mistakes. While not condoning mistakes, especially serious ones, it is important to understand that the normal mistakes made in parenthood do not *cause* children to do what they do as adults. One parent said, "But didn't my mistakes cause my child to become a drug addict?" If parental mistakes, per se, caused drug addiction, all children would become addicts because all parents make a lot of mistakes. I am speaking of common parental mistakes, not abuse. Severe abuse may increase the propensity toward drug use. However, the truth still holds that most parents are not abusive and parents rarely teach children to use drugs; in fact, they almost always teach them *not* to use drugs.

One child may choose to use drugs while another child in the same family may choose to go on a mission, even though he may have been treated exactly the same as the first child. The difference lies in how the people respond to their circumstances.

OUR SPIRITUAL BAROMETER: HOW WE RELATE TO OTHERS

Mormon spoke clearly of the relationship between our spirituality and how we relate to others when he said, "Wherefore, I would speak unto you that are of the church, that are the peaceable followers of Christ, and that have obtained a sufficient hope by which ye can enter into the rest of the Lord, from this time henceforth until ye shall rest with him in Heaven." (Moroni 7:3.) Mormon is speaking to members who are peaceable followers of Christ, for he said, "I judge these things of you because of your peaceable walk with the children of men."

How we relate to others, our "peaceable walk," is a direct manifestation of our attitude toward others. Walking peaceably with others, in a spirit of love, is healing. When we attempt to manipulate, we lack love and are at that moment as "sounding brass, or a tinkling cymbal." (1 Corinthians 13:1.)

However, this doesn't mean "peace at any price" or "outer peace at the expense of inner peace." This is a hard concept for many codependents to understand. Some conclude that because they should be loving, they should still allow others to walk on them, take advantage of them, and manipulate them. This is not the case. The words of Joseph Smith can help us find this balance, for he said, "Don't be limited in your views with regard to your neighbor's virtue, but beware of self-righteousness, and be limited in the estimate of your own virtues, and not think yourselves more righteous than others; you must enlarge your souls towards each other, if you would do like Jesus, and carry your fellow-creatures to Abraham's bosom." (TPJS, p. 228.)

CODEPENDENTS ARE VULNERABLE TO APOSTATES, MANIPULATORS, AND SCAM ARTISTS.

One aspect of codependency is the increased vulnerability to being influenced by those who criticize the Church and its teachings. Because of their need to please and not offend others, codependents are very susceptible to being deceived by negative messages from apostates. How easy it is to pick up the judgmental habit the Prophet Joseph Smith warned about when he said, "We are full of selfishness; the devil flatters us that we are very righteous, when we are feeding on the faults of others." (TPJS, p. 241.)

Those who manipulate others can expertly spot a person who is overly sensitive to what others think and who can be easily manipulated. They use this insight to manipulate the person into listening to and then believing their destructive messages. They take advantage of negatives they observe in the Church and teach that negatives are bound to weaken or destroy a testimony. This breaks the hearts of family and friends who recognize what is happening to the codependent, and he later feels deep remorse when he realizes how he was duped. Truly, as someone said, "The most powerful muscle in the body is the tongue because it is the only muscle that can break a heart."

Scam artists and apostates find fault anywhere and then use this information to manipulate others. Even the Lord's Church isn't perfect, so they find faults in the Church and its leadership and point them out. For instance, not all the sacrament meetings in the Church are the model of reverence. (Is that a tactful understatement?) This fact gives them something negative to point out. Neil J. Flinders taught a great truth that helps us come to terms with this problem when he said, "We need a testimony strong enough to survive *in spite of,* not because of, our experiences in the Church."

Too many codependents are also vulnerable to scams and charlatans. They buy things they don't need because "expert" salespersons can easily spot and manipulate them. Again, "Let no man deceive you with vain words." (Ephesians 5:6.)

A related concern for codependents is their tendency to misinterpret the statements of Church leaders. For example, one of my favorite quotes by the Prophet Joseph Smith is "Never be discouraged. If I were sunk in the lowest pit in Nova Scotia with the Rocky Mountains piled on top of me I would hang on, exercise faith, and keep up good courage and I'd come out on top." (George A. Smith's Journal, quoted by Prestion Nibley, *Deseret News*, 12 Mar. 1950, p. 16.) When this quote is shared with codependents, instead of hearing something that motivates them not to be discouraged, they say to themselves, "I'm never supposed to be discouraged? Well, I can't do that. I just cannot follow what the Prophet Joseph Smith said. What kind of a member of the Church am I?"

Codependents may misinterpret a lot of statements using black and white thinking, which is a form of perfectionism.

Events, people themselves, mistakes, even personal successes are seen as all or nothing, all good or all bad. Black and white thinking causes a lot of problems for codependents until they learn that all good people sin, make mistakes, experience bad events, and experience personal failures and as well as personal successes.

 *Chapter 5*

Applying Gospel Principles
to Heal Codependency

Many years ago, in a Christmas Eve editorial, the *Standard Examiner* showed a drawing of a man surrounded by dozens of presents. The caption said, "Now let's see, have I forgotten anyone?" In the background, almost hidden among the presents, was the sad, forgotten face of the Savior.

We cannot forget the Savior in our healing process, for he alone can totally free us from the bondage of codependency. "If the Son therefore shall make you free, ye shall be free indeed." (John 8:36.) This freedom begins when we understand that he loves us as children of God. Elder Neal Maxwell said, "If we know who we are and whose we are, this belonging and acceptance results in much less need for mortal acceptance and acclaim." (*Not My Will, But Thine*, p. 94.) Understanding this does not detract from the help available from other people. Many times the Savior works through other mortals to give us the help we need.

To be healed of codependency, we need the Spirit to help us know what applies to our lives individually. With the Lord's help, our healing will be especially tailored to our individual needs for our best good in the long run. Just as a priesthood blessing may bring about various degrees of physical healing, there can also be varying degrees of healing of codependency at various times in our lives.

For our long-range healing, the Lord has provided for us the Plan of Salvation. In a Relief Society lesson, Anita

Bennett, a lover of words, asked, "Do you know about the word 'salvation'? There is a word in English that will give you a clue. For instance, what does 'salve' do? Several in the room responded, "It heals." She continued, "The Plan of Salvation . . . is a plan of healing, of wholeness . . . of holiness." The first and most important meaning that Webster's Dictionary gives for the word "save" is "to rescue, or preserve from harm or danger, keep or to remove from damage or injury." The gospel of Jesus Christ does provide healing and rescue from danger or injury, even the kind caused by codependency.

The first principles of the gospel heal us. Joseph Smith said, "I advise all to go on to perfection, and search deeper and deeper into the mysteries of Godliness." (TPJS p. 364.) There is a difference between the mysteries of Godliness and the "mysteries" which we are to avoid. An Institute of Religion instructor taught me that the mysteries of Godliness are faith in Jesus Christ, repentance, baptism, and the Gift of the Holy Ghost. *These* mysteries can provide us a foundation as we heal.

The Lord spoke to Thomas B. Marsh, a past president of the Quorum of the Twelve Apostles, about gospel healing when he said, "I know thy heart, and have heard thy prayers concerning thy brethren. Be not partial towards them in love above many others, but let thy love be for them as for thyself; and let thy love abound unto all men, and unto all who love my name. And pray for thy brethren of the Twelve. Admonish them sharply for my name's sake, and let them be admonished for all their sins, and be ye faithful before me unto my name. And after their temptation, and much tribulation, behold I, the Lord, will feel after them and if they harden not their hearts, and stiffen not their necks against me, they shall be converted, and I will heal them. (D&C 112:11-13.)

In this scripture, the Lord is teaching us to love others, to have a commitment to righteousness, and to overcome temptations and trials by drawing close to the Lord. If we draw close to him when we are hurt, the Lord will draw close to us. This will promote conversion and healing in our lives. This conversion consists of knowing more deeply that this is the Lord's restored Church, and of experiencing a more complete knowledge of the atonement. We need a more complete belief that the atonement works in our own lives and that it can heal us. This healing can be physical, emotional, and/or spiritual; this means that the atonement can heal codependency. We are all tempted and we all sin, but the day will come when our most important priority will be to become clean and free of our sins. This will help us experience deeper joy.

Instead of pursuing this path to healing and peace, the adversary wants us to seek carnal, material goals or to center our lives on pleasing others. "And Adam and Eve blessed the name of God, and they made all things known unto their sons and their daughters. And Satan came among them saying: I am also a son of God; and he commanded them saying: Believe it not; and they believed it not, and they loved Satan more than God. And men began from that time forth to be carnal sensual, and devilish." (Moses 5:12-13.)

King Benjamin taught his people about Christ and the healing power of Christ's atonement with this result: "And they had viewed themselves in their own carnal state, even less than the dust of the earth. And they all cried aloud with one voice, saying: O have mercy, and apply the atoning blood of Christ that we may receive forgiveness of our sins, and our hearts may be purified; for we believe in Jesus Christ, the Son of God, who created heaven and earth, and all things; who shall come down among the children of men." (Mosiah 4:2.)

But how can we know we are experiencing the healing of which these scriptures speak? Below are twenty ways we can know whether we are experiencing healing from codependency:

1. We are learning to use the gospel to assess our progress.

Using the gospel, we can be healed of our ACOA or dysfunctional issues as we gain more awareness of our thoughts, and learn to identify and deal with our feelings in Christlike ways. We need to be aware that healing occurs on three different levels: the level of thoughts, the level of feelings, and on a spiritual level through Christ.

Thoughts

Our thoughts are very important, for as we think, so are we. (Proverbs 23:7.) How we think determines our happiness. While essential, working on the thought level can only go so far to heal us. Some people try to solve all their problems in their heads; but healing also requires that we explore and work through our feelings. We may need the help of a church leader or a counselor to help us understand and apply healing principles in order to overcome and let go of past negative feelings.

Feelings

It is possible to intellectually understand a problem so well that we can help others understand and overcome the same problem, and yet do nothing to overcome the problem ourselves. We can teach others correct principles about codependency and yet prevent our own healing by denying our deep feelings that lead us to enable others to avoid the consequences of their codependent behavior or to rescue them from such consequences.

A codependent woman may not understand her *own* feelings at all as she considers marrying a man who abuses her, yet she may understand intellectually and be able to verbalize the reasons why she should not marry him. Still her own codependent feelings may prevent her from acting on her knowledge. Because of her own unresolved feelings she may go ahead and marry someone totally wrong for her in spite of the fact that she can help other women avoid making that same mistake.

We must work through many of our problems at the feeling level, for answers to personal questions often come from our feelings. In fact, we become confused when we deny a real or honest feeling. Sorting out feelings does away with confusion. Many codependent problems are based in feelings, and learning to recognize and understand these feelings can promote healing.

Spiritual Healing through Christ

In addition to understanding our thoughts and feelings, we can eliminate pain through a change of heart that can permanently transform our lives. This is what the scriptures refer to as the sacrifice of a broken heart and a contrite spirit. (See 3 Nephi 12:19; D&C 59:8.) As we come unto Christ, he promises us that our burdens can be lifted and that they will become light. Our codependency is healed as we seek to please our Heavenly Father and Christ. As President Ezra Taft Benson said, "Men and women who turn their lives over to God will find out that he can make a lot more out of their lives than they can. He will deepen their joys, expand their vision, quicken their minds, strengthen their muscles, lift their spirits, multiply their blessings, increase their opportunities, comfort their souls, raise up friends and pour out peace." (*Speeches of the Year*, 1974, Provo, Utah: BYU Press, p. 310.)

We cannot overcome our weaknesses and sins on our own. This is a spiritual process for which we require the Lord's help to be healed. Jesus taught, "I am the true vine, and my Father is the husbandman. . . . Abide in me, and I in you. As the branch cannot bear fruit of itself, except it abide in the vine; no more can ye, except ye abide in me. I am the vine, ye are the branches; He that abideth in me, and I in him, the same bringeth forth much fruit: for without me ye can do nothing." (John 15: 1, 4,5.)

2. We are learning to give ourselves credit for progress.

We experience healing from codependency and related problems as we learn to give ourselves appropriate credit for our progress. We can become discouraged about our progress simply because we fail to give ourselves appropriate credit. Since the adversary wants us to fail, if he cannot discourage us through sin, he will try to encourage us to judge ourselves too harshly.

A   B   C

If we are at point A, and our goal is to get to point C, but we only make it to point B, the adversary wants us to beat ourselves up for not reaching our goal. He knows this will discourage us and that it can possibly even cause us to digress and give up. However, we can thwart these efforts of the adversary to defeat us. If we give ourselves credit for progress we have made, we will feel joy and increased self-esteem. We also will also constantly feel humble because we recognize our dependence upon the Lord for our success and progress.

3. We are progressing on the spiritual growth continuum.

Listed on the next page are three levels of spiritual growth. It can be helpful to us as we assess whether we are developing telestial, terrestrial, or celestial attitudes as we grow spiritually.

When we have judgmental and impatient attitudes with others and when we use a checklist-approach to living gospel principles those are signs that we need to grow spiritually. All of us have probably been at those levels at some time in our lives. I know of a new convert who wanted his bishop to turn off all the drinking fountains on fast Sunday so the members could not drink water on that day. Today, this same convert is a very spiritual church leader who is embarrassed by his former attitude. A real indicator of our spiritual growth is our willingness to be more accepting of others without manipulating them or allowing them to manipulate us.

Telestial Spirituality	Terrestrial Spirituality	Celestial Spirituality
• Fanatical—critical of self and others	• More accepting of self and others.	• Christlike love of self and others.
• "People have been controlling me."	• "I am learning how to communicate without controlling or preaching to others."	• Communicate with others with love.
• "Now, no one will ever control me. I will let them know when they are wrong, etc."	• Learning, "I am OK and you are OK. As I feel love for me, I feel caring for you and your feelings. I treat you better due to my empathy."	• Communicate with attitude that "everyone is of equal value, regardless of one's race, religion, sex, job, church calling, etc."
• Checklist mentality of church activity.		
• "I am good if I attend church, pay my tithing, etc."	• "I am learning that how I treat others is one of the most important parts of the gospel, which is an evidence of how well I am living the gospel."	• "I treat you better due to my love for you, myself, and the Lord."
• "How I treat people is not important, especially if they disagree with me and give me grief."		• "I have learned I can give love, and still be assertive, and challenge others as needed."
• "My anger is really righteous indignation."	• "I am also learning that this also means I need never allow anyone to mistreat me."	

4. We are learning to fulfill our needs appropriately with gospel service.

Healing comes as we learn how to fulfill our needs as the gospel teaches. The fruits of living the gospel on the level of Christlike love are joy and peace. When we attempt to fulfill our needs in inappropriate ways, ways that disregard the gospel, the fruits are remorse, pain, and an increased need for love and acceptance.

Codependency is healed as we learn to fulfill our needs through the Spirit, a process dealt with in the hymn "A Poor Wayfaring Man of Grief." This hymn teaches the spirit of Christlike service which involves love. The man in the hymn approached people as if they were Christ. As we feel the spirit of this kind of service, we experience healing from codependency.

5. We are experiencing healing as we study the scriptures and have personal prayers.

One sister complained that whenever she went to her bishop for help, he counseled her to "pray and read the scriptures." She wanted *more* than that.

She needed to learn that the joy and peace we experience from immersing ourselves in prayer and the scriptures helps us be healed of codependency. Whatever "more" she wanted (a counseling situation, for example) would be more effective and appropriate if she were also being obedient to the counsel to pray and read the scriptures daily.

We cannot successfully survive or progress spiritually without prayer, the scriptures, the guidance of the Holy Spirit, and a close relationship with our Heavenly Father. Brigham Young taught this in a discourse when he said, "Live so that you will know the moment the Spirit of the Almighty is grieved within you." (From a Discourse delivered by Brigham Young on 13 August 1871.) The Lord has counseled us in D&C 88:118 to study and seek learning out of the best books—and appropriate books *can* be extremely helpful to our growth. Still, scripture study combined with meaningful prayer provide strength and peace that can be obtained in no other way. It is as someone has said, "A Bible that's falling apart usually belongs to someone who isn't." This statement could be equally applicable to all the standard works.

Reading and pondering the scriptures helps us develop and maintain within our hearts a childlike teachable attitude—the basis of the "broken heart and [the] contrite spirit" required by the Savior. (3 Nephi 9:20, 2 Nephi 2:7.) This attitude provides inner strength, joy, hope, and peace in the midst of trials, and also deters us and our families from sin. "Behold, verily, verily, I say unto you, ye must watch and pray always, lest ye enter into temptation; for Satan desireth to have you that he may sift you as wheat. Therefore ye must always pray unto the Father in my name." (3 Nephi 18:18-19.)

As President Ezra Taft Benson taught, "Prayer keeps you from sinning, and sinning keeps you from praying." (Dew, Sheri L., *Ezra Taft Benson, an Autobiography*, Deseret Book, 1987, Salt Lake City, Utah, p. 151.)

6. We are able to detach from the problems of others.

Detaching does not mean withdrawing love and support from those who have problems. It means that we do not accept responsibility for others' problems since they are not our stewardship. We can learn to detach ourselves from others' problems in a healthy way instead of withdrawing from a person in need.

Some misunderstand the detaching concept and think it means giving up and withdrawing. It is actually the opposite. When we detach ourselves from others' problems, we continue to provide love, warmth, emotional support, and caring, but we simply leave the person's free agency intact and keep our own free agency intact. Thus, we are living responsibly ourselves and allowing the other person to live responsibly also.

7. We are learning to grow from our trials.

I have had many trials, caused mostly by my own mistakes. The Lord's help, his comfort, and the love I have felt during prayer and priesthood blessings have kept me going. Hope can remain as a bright beacon when the present seems dark and the mistakes of the past become an almost unbearable weight.

Being codependent is an example of such a trial. As we search the scriptures, we realize our trials can become blessings, for "the trial of your faith, being much more precious than of gold that perisheth." (1 Peter 1:7.) "See that ye be not troubled: for all these things must come to pass." (Matthew 24:6.) We will all experience trials to determine whether we are "willing to submit to all things which the Lord seeth fit to inflict upon [us]." (Mosiah 3:19.) Peace for all of us comes as we pass through our own Gethsemanes, and as we follow the Savior. "If any man will come after me, let him deny himself, and take up his cross, and follow me." (Matthew 16:24.)

Lynn M. Roundy said of this scripture that there were three expectations: "First, he must 'deny himself,' or cease to be motivated by the things of the world and to achieve mastery over himself; second, the Savior asked that we each take up our own 'cross'. . . . The 'cross' then, becomes the heavy 'burden' of our lives—our trials and sufferings; and third, after getting the cross shouldered, we are asked to follow Him. Follow Him where? To Calvary! That is where He took His cross. Picking up the 'cross' is not necessarily the end of our torments, but perhaps only the beginning . . . 'And he that taketh not his cross, and followeth after me, is not worthy of me'(Matthew 10:38.)" (Roundy, Lynn M. "Your Own Crown of Thorns." *AMCAP Journal*, July, 1983, pp. 15-16.)

Elder Neal A. Maxwell asked, "What then, are some of the skills and strengths . . . which enable us to lift and then to carry the cross? First, we must realize that the weight of the cross is great enough without our carrying burdens that we could jettison through the process of repentance. It is so much more difficult for us to carry the cross when our back is already bent with the burdens of bad behavior. Second, the cross is something we cannot shoulder and then stand still with. The cross is easier to carry if we keep moving. Action and service happily require enough of our attention that the sagging of self-pity can be avoided. Third, we must realize, finally, that we can only contemplate the cross just so long: rhetoric will not raise it. It must soon either be taken up or turned away from!" (Maxwell, Neal A. "Speeches of the Year," Provo: Brigham Young University Press, 1976, p. 259.)

As we respond to our trials by drawing close to the Lord, we become more sensitive to the Spirit and experience a deeper motivation to repent of our unrepented sins, both past and present. If we draw close to the Lord, then our desire to please the Lord becomes most important. As we draw near to the Lord and feel that he is pleased with our progress, we then find peace.

As we experience this peace, we then move in one of two directions: we experience deeper peace when we give the Lord the credit, or we curtail our growth by taking credit unto ourselves for our progress. The prophet Zenos spoke of this in his allegory of the tame and the wild olive trees.

The olive trees were not doing well in spite of the best efforts of the Lord of the vineyard, so the servant said, "Is it not the loftiness of thy vineyard—have not the branches thereof overcome the roots which are good? . . . the branches have overcome the roots thereof . . . taking strength unto themselves. Behold, I say is not this the cause that the trees of thy vineyard have become corrupted?" (Jacob 5:48.) The prophets have warned us about this pride, which can destroy our peace.

The Lord wants us to respond to our trials and suffering by drawing closer to him. As the trial passes, the pattern of turning to him will hopefully remain a part of our lives and we will be open to learn the lessons from each trial. "God pity those who cannot say: 'Not mine, but thine,' who only pray 'Let this cup pass,' and cannot see the purpose in Gethsemane." (Mossison, *Masterpieces of Religious Verse,* Harper and Brothers, 1948, p. 184.)

Anne Morrow Lindberg understood this when she said, "I do not believe that sheer suffering teaches. If suffering alone taught, all the world would be wise, since everyone suffers. To suffering must be added mourning, understanding, patience, love, openness, and the willingness to remain vulnerable." (*Time,* 5 February 1973.)

The Lord will help us reach our righteous goals. We are taught to "search diligently, pray always, and be believing, and all things shall work together for your good, if ye walk uprightly." (D&C 90:24.)

8. We are experiencing the healing aspects of love.

Love and fear are opposites

Love and fear are opposite emotions. Insecurity and fear are the same. Insecurity is a fear of being rejected or hurt. An insecure person perceives the cause of insecurity to be outside himself, when it actually comes from within. When they are feeling insecure, many codependents feel fear or hurt and then feel angry, victimized, or like martyrs. They then become unable to feel love. As we learn to think secure thoughts, we experience and feel love more easily.

Sin for many codependents arises from an attempt to fulfill a need for love in an inappropriate way and to compulsively seek love from others. When we expect others to fill inner needs that can be filled only by our righteous efforts to repent and serve the Lord, we always remain frustrated.

When we seek love from others *inappropriately*, we "fall in *need*," we do not "fall in *love*." Some people attempt to find substitutes for love through such things as sex, food, drugs, pornography, or physical pleasures, but these things never fulfill a codependent's need for love. The need is filled as we learn to love self and sense God's love. Without these two essential foundation blocks, instead of finding fulfillment, the person only experiences an increased need for love. For some, this cycle leads to inactivity in the Church and even to hatred of the truth and self. This spiritually self-destructive cycle of self-hatred can lead to more sin, which leads to more anger, and to additional sin. A deep need for love, a deep hurt, anger, and self-hate can turn to hate for others, even for the Lord.

Caught in this negative cycle, some people feel victimized, seeing another person as the cause of their negative feelings; some people even seek an affair as a desperate attempt to find love. They usually deny any responsibility for these actions. The telestial kingdom will be a "hell" for those who realize too late why they were turning to sinful behavior and what was lost in the process. (Mosiah 3:27.)

Codependent healing comes from within when we feel the Lord's love for us and feel love from ourselves. This love helps us think secure thoughts so we can have peace.

We can love and serve the Lord with all our hearts

We can love the Lord with all our "Heart, with all [our] might mind, and strength." (D&C 59:5.) As we do, it heals us; however, we cannot sin with all our hearts. Sin divides us, creates a conflict and a schism in our personalities. Living righteously creates a healing wholeness that is found in no other way. Cecil B. DeMille said, "God does not contradict himself. He did not create man and then, as an afterthought, impose upon him a set of arbitrary restrictive rules. He made man free and then gave him the commandments to keep him free. We cannot break the ten commandments. We can only break ourselves against them—or else, by keeping them, rise through them to the fullness of freedom under God." (quoted by Richard L. Evans in an address "The Ultimate Objective," delivered on the CBS Radio "Church of the Air," 11 October 1959.)

Love is the gospel of Jesus Christ

Some codependents become so intense in living a gospel checklist, trying to "do it all," that they never realize that being kind, patient, and loving with others is the heart of the gospel. Task orientation and the need to perform to "earn worth" are significant contributors to the bondage of the codependent. It is a significant healing day for codependents when they realize that they can be appropriately loving with others without feeling a need to do something to deserve or get love in return—when they can put their checklists aside and just *be* loving. It is also healing when they learn how to set boundaries that keep others from manipulating or mistreating them as they provide love.

As we experience the healing benefits of receiving love from the Lord and giving him love in return, a new application of gospel principles begins to develop in our lives. We all need this experience, for we are all sent to this earth with the hope that we will learn the joy of becoming loving so we can provide Christlike service and fulfill our individual missions. If we were raised in a home that provided this kind of love, we will learn this more easily. If we were raised in a dysfunctional home, the Lord will still help us to fulfill our responsibility to become loving.

The wounds of dysfunctional homes and codependency are not generally healed quickly. But allowing ourselves time to grow while staying close to the Lord will heal. The results are worth the struggle and the wait.

There is a difference between love and trust

A codependent's healing requires that he understand the difference between love and trust. David O. McKay said, "It is a greater compliment to be trusted than to be loved." Love can be given unconditionally, but trust has to be earned. I am sure the Lord loves Satan, but can he trust him?

As codependents learn to give love to others, they must not confuse this love with trust. They may still love people who have mistreated them, but appropriately not trust them. Those who violate another's trust may later try to manipulate others by saying: "If you really loved me, you would trust me," or "It is your problem that you don't trust me," or "If you weren't sick [or immature or LDS or codependent] you would trust me." Nothing is farther from the truth. Winning back someone's trust may take a *long time*, and if the slowly building trust is violated again, it can take much longer. Sometimes there is not enough time in this life to build back the trust.

A codependent does not necessarily have a "problem" because she needs sufficient time to build trust. Anyone who sincerely wants to have a trusting relationship with a codependent will provide the necessary time, without manipulating others. This person may also need to understand that the inability to provide trust may not be due to any part of the present relationship, but it may be due to past negative experiences in relationships. A counselor can help a codependent work through these issues in order to again learn to trust.

We can become more loving

Codependents need to know in their hearts that the Lord loves them. Then when they make mistakes, or even sin, they will know the Lord still loves them unconditionally.

The Lord does not excuse our behavior, but he does always love us.

Matthew Cowley learned how to give non-codependent love. President George Albert Smith said of Matthew Cowley at his funeral that "He loved everyone because he could see the good within them. He did not look upon sin with the least degree of allowance, but he loved the sinner because he knew that God was love, and that it is God's love that regenerates human souls and may, by that process, transform the sinner into a saint. Maybe there are sinners who mistook his love for respect. He didn't respect the sinner, but he loved him. I am sure that love found response in the hearts and in the lives of those whom he loved."

Love also prevents more codependent mistakes, even sins. In 1 Peter 4:8, the Apostle Peter said, "And above all things have fervent charity among yourselves: for charity shall cover the multitude of sins." The Prophet Joseph Smith corrected the word "cover" by saying that "love *preventeth* a multitude of sins."

We need the pure love of Christ in order to grow and develop because "charity suffereth long, and is kind; charity envieth not; charity vaunteth not itself, is not puffed up, Doth not behave itself unseemly . . . thinketh no evil; Rejoiceth not in iniquity, but rejoiceth in the truth; Beareth all things, believeth all things, hopeth all things, endureth all things. Charity never faileth." (1 Corinthians 13:4-8.) What more could we ask for?

We need to be loved and to give love unconditionally

William Glasser taught that we all have two needs: to love and be loved, and to feel worthwhile about ourselves and others. (Glasser, William, *Reality Therapy*) To help prevent codependency, our children need to know and feel they are loved unconditionally. Some youth rebel when they feel that someone important in their life does not love them; and many conclude they do not deserve to be loved. Others "set up" situations so that parents (or any authority figure) will become angry with them so that they will have an excuse to do something negative that they want to do.

A teenager may know that a certain word will bring rage from a parent. The teenager starts an argument by saying the word, the parent becomes angry as predicted, and the teenager does what he wanted to do (such as run away from home), but he now blames his parents for his actions. Some take hurt feelings and turn them into rebellion and say, "I'll do as I please." Some focus on negatives, turn them into anger, push others away, then feel justified in doing so.

For codependents who struggle with the commandment to love others, it can be helpful to understand that it is our own problems that prevent us from feeling love from the Lord or for others. Someone has said, "It's not what others *do* that make them unlovable to us, but rather *how we judge their actions*." This is tough doctrine, but as we feel more secure and think more secure thoughts, we feel love from ourselves, from others, and from the Lord. (This doctrine does *not* mean, however, that in cases in which another's actions constitute mistreatment or abuse, we should allow that person to continue abusing or mistreating us. Priesthood leaders or appropriate counselors need to be consulted in these cases and the abuse needs to be stopped.)

Codependents can experience the healing that comes by seeking approval from the Lord rather than from others. When we know the Lord loves us, we can more easily seek his approval and feel less need for the approval of others. Love does change people, or at least provides the atmosphere in which they can choose to change if they want to. Love may be applied to the codependency continuum as seen on the next page.

Selfish	Codependent	Gospel Service
Has no love for self or others. Cares only for self, but verbalizes love if needed, to benefit self. No love, only manipulation. Attempts to control others.	Struggles to provide love to self and others. Questions whether he deserves love. Serves with hope that he will receive the love he desperately needs from others. Allows himself to be controlled by others.	Loves self and others. Provides others a Christlike healing love. Receives healing love from the Lord, provides love to others through service. Does not control or manipulate others. Does not allow others to control or manipulate her.

We seek the divine nature to provide healing love

Healing comes through the Lord Jesus Christ. The Apostle Peter said, "Whereby are given unto us exceeding great and precious promises; that by these ye might be partakers of the divine nature, having escaped the corruption that is in the world through lust. And beside this, giving all diligence, add to your faith virtue; and to virtue knowledge; And to knowledge temperance; and to temperance patience; and to patience godliness; And to godliness brotherly kindness; and to brotherly kindness charity. For if these things be in you, and abound, they make you that ye shall neither be barren nor unfruitful in the knowledge of our Lord Jesus Christ. But he that lacketh these things is blind, and cannot see afar off, and hath forgotten that he was purged from his old sins." (2 Peter 1:4-9.)

This idea might be stated in modern language like this: "Love is where it's at!" (For more on the healing power of love, see Chapter Five in *The New Stress Reduction for Mormons.*)

9. We are learning to respond positively to appropriate guilt (we allow it to motivate us to repentance) and we are recognizing and ridding ourselves of inappropriate guilt.

Guilt is the great destroyer of codependents because they inappropriately blame themselves for whatever is wrong. They somehow believe they are responsible for other people and circumstances over which they have no control and believe they should be able to "fix" everything. This mindset leads to inappropriately feeling guilty for things we are not responsible for. It is also inappropriate to feel continuing guilt when we sincerely repent of mistakes we *are* responsible for yet continue to beat ourselves up and feel guilty (even though we say we believe in the atonement.)

We can also be negatively impacted by appropriate guilt (feeling bad for actual wrongdoings) when we sin and then fail to completely repent—when, instead of recognizing our guilt as a valid indicator of our need to repent, we try to feel whole and deny our appropriate guilt. Guilt divides us spiritually and some people try to feel whole by avoiding its pain. Denying feelings of pain can become a deeply ingrained habit for codependents; it is an obvious danger to use that approach with guilt. Many who drift from or fight the truth do just that. Guilt can be stuffed in so deeply that we don't feel it at all. Or it can be intellectualized so much that we can convince ourselves (and others) that there is no need for the guilt. Korihor, the Anti-Christ in the Book of Mormon, is an example of this. (See Alma Chapter 30.) If those who fight the truth can dupe themselves into believing that the truth is not the truth, then they eliminate the need for guilt.

For example, Some codependents use the gospel as an excuse to avoid looking honestly at themselves. One very insecure, obnoxious, self-centered, codependent girl believed that others did not like her because she was a Mormon who was living her religion. When her bishop and counselor confronted her with her own responsibility for her selfish, obnoxious behavior, she concluded that her bishop and all counselors were uninspired or they would not say such things to someone living her religion. This denial prevented her from feeling appropriate guilt, which would lead her to repent or change her behaviors.

To better understand the spiritual and emotional ways in which some codependents struggle with guilt, consider the example of Suzette, who became sexually involved with her boyfriend and was feeling guilty. She visited Sam, a liberal counselor who believed in getting rid of both the inappropriate *and* the appropriate guilt psychologically. The following conversation ensued:

Suzette: I'm here because I feel guilty about sleeping with my boyfriend. I want to get rid of this guilt.

Sam: Well, why are you feeling so guilty? That is what's wrong with your church. It makes you feel guilty too much of the time. I can help you get rid of your guilt very quickly.

Thankfully, this approach is not practiced by many counselors, LDS or not. But in our example, Suzette is being taught that there is a way to eliminate her appropriate guilt without repentance. That is not the truth. As a codependent, Suzette will grow spiritually if she realizes that when she sins, she *should* feel appropriate guilt that leads to sincere repentance. This guilt can be eliminated only through Christ's atonement and her sincere repentance. Trying to eliminate the source of appropriate guilt does not eliminate the guilt, for it is always there until repented of.

But codependents have another problem: their inappropriate guilt is often subtly attached to their appropriate guilt. Separating the two becomes very difficult and confusing. Appropriate guilt, when sins are repented of, should be gone, but how can codependents learn to identify and get rid of inappropriate guilt?

Inappropriate guilt is a result of feeling unduly responsible, being too hard on ourselves, or having expectations that are too high. Few codependents realize that their expectations are too high because they have learned to succeed by performing extremely well. Other people do not understand how difficult it is for typical "perfectionistic codependents" to lower their expectations. The very thought creates a fear of failure that is equivalent to requiring them to have perfect children by tomorrow. They believe it just cannot be done. The whole basis for their worth may be tied up with performing well. Telling them to lower their expectations seems to them to be saying that you don't have to perform well. They just can't buy it. Yet unrealistic expectations absolutely set us up for discouragement and unhappiness.

One common unrealistic expectation is that if we live the gospel, everyone will like us. Yet, even the Savior was hated by many.

Some codependents make an otherwise realistic expectations become unrealistic by expecting to accomplish a two- or three-hour task (i.e. clean the house, write a paper, or write a report for the boss) in less than an hour. Then when it takes two hours to complete, instead of adjusting the goal and giving themselves credit for getting it done, they beat themselves up with guilt for not being able to do the impossible by completing the task within their original time expectation. (For more on expectations see Chapter Nine in *The New Stress Reduction for Mormons*.)

Unrealistic expectations that result in inappropriate guilt are part of Satan's deceptions. There are serious risks that come with them. Because of their dysfunctional issues, codependents can become so overburdened by excessive inappropriate guilt that they do not sort it out and deal with appropriate guilt by repenting, as the gospel teaches. Instead, they may accept psychological "quick-fixes" or invitations to sinful behavior that promise relief from the terrible burden and guilt they feel. This pattern explains why so many codependents are so susceptible to anti-Mormon or gospel-destroying beliefs, especially if those beliefs are clearly concealed by a guilt-reducing lifestyle.

Recognizing and admitting when we have been deceived can be a great challenge.

Korihor so strongly denied his deception that he had to be struck dumb by a prophet of God before he was convinced. But he then wrote: "Yea, and I always knew that there was a God. But behold, the devil hath deceived me." (Alma 30:52, 53.) He said he was told to teach "There is no God; . . . And I taught his words because they were pleasing unto the carnal mind; and I taught them, even until I had much success, insomuch that I verily believed that they were true . . ." Yet, even after this confession, Alma knew the heart of Korihor, for he told him, "If this curse should be taken from thee thou wouldst again lead away the hearts of this people." (Alma 30:54.) Such is the state of many of those who would lead a codependent away from the Lord's Church or from any truth contained therein.

If this does not happen to the codependent, it does happen to many who are willing to deceive the codependent. In the case of Korihor, because of the power of God through the Prophet Alma upon Korihor, "They were all convinced of the wickedness of Korihor; therefore they were all converted again unto the Lord." (Alma 30:58.) In our day, codependents can prevent this from happening in their lives by being aware of their vulnerability and staying close to the Lord and his church.

10. We are learning not to worry.

Codependents often confuse caring with worrying. They believe that the more they worry, the more they show they truly care. This "Martha" mentality of gospel living and service was identified by the Savior when he said, "Martha, Martha, thou art careful and troubled about many things: But one thing is needful: and Mary hath chosen that good part, which shall not be taken away from her." What had Mary chosen? It was to sit at the feet of Jesus and "hear his word." (Luke 10: 41,42.)

Healing comes when, rather than fretting and worrying, we use the words and feelings that come from the Spirit of the Lord and the scriptures to calm us. Worrying is a habit that we choose to continue; at times, it is even a tool of the adversary that destroys peace. Faith that life will eventually turn out for the best in spite of life's difficulties can give us the strength to overcome the habit of worrying.

11. We are recognizing our own self-worth.

We experience healing when we can finally make a mistake without feeling a need to beat ourselves up. We are overcoming our old non-gospel belief that mistakes decrease our worth. This does not mean we ever excuse sin, but rather that we can finally see our worth as unconditional—that our worth is not decreased by mistakes and sins we repent of.

As we follow this process of becoming more and more sure of our individual worth, we experience healing because we are applying gospel teachings rather than worldly teachings. The gospel teaches us that we are worthwhile because we are children of God; there are no qualifiers. Everyone has worth. The world teaches us that we are worthwhile only if we perform well, and that the better we perform the more worthwhile we become. Realizing the difference between what the gospel teaches and what the world teaches can help us to avoid destructive self-put-downs. Our self-esteem is as strong as is our realization that we are of worth unconditionally. As one sister said, "I understood this in my head for years, but it finally came into my heart. For the first time in my life I could feel worthwhile and feel constant love from the Lord even when I made mistakes. That was a big step for me." We can generalize this idea to mean that others are also worthwhile unconditionally—even when *they* make mistakes.

If we could only understand the worth we knew in the preexistence, that alone would take us a long way toward healing. From the journal of a recovering codependent we read:

> I learned that I had been keeping myself busy in order to avoid negative feelings, but when I slowed down and faced

these feelings, I felt I was not acceptable enough to be loved by anyone. I wanted to run, to get so busy that I could not feel it. But I was led by the Lord's Spirit to realize that the real me was a person loved by the Lord even before coming to this earth—a person with healing self-worth who is loved and lovable.

Negative messages learned during this earth life piled so much garbage upon this healthy center that I hardly knew it was really there. My sins, my dysfunctional home, my codependency issues, and the message from society that my performance equals my worth all blinded me.

As I rediscovered my real self and *felt* deep feelings of self-worth, I no longer felt a need to impress others. With this core of inner self-worth, I found calmness, peace, and love. My former needs were disappearing: the need to be right, to blame others, to change others so I could be happy. I was astounded at how much time and energy I had spent dealing with garbage, trying to please, creating defenses . . . just being codependent. My new goal is to remain in touch with my real self, my spiritual being, so my healing can continue. My relationships with others will never be the same because I realize we all have this core person of worth and love, and that all of us can come to realize it is there and to experience this same healing.

Healing also comes as we understand that worthiness is a result of how well we keep the commandments and live the gospel. The adversary teaches us that when we commit a sin, we have lost not only our worthiness, but also our worth. The gospel clearly separates worth from worthiness. It teaches us that worthiness through keeping the commandments is very different from unconditional self-worth. We are unworthy when we are involved in sin by doing something morally wrong or breaking a commandment, for example. We are unworthy when we do things that prevent us from having a temple recommend; however, we still have self-worth. Through wrong actions, we may lose blessings, privileges, progress, and exaltation, but we do not lose our worth. Understanding this helps us fight off the messages of the adversary that can completely discourage and destroy us. Many bishops have helped excommunicated members find the courage to come back by helping them realize that their self-worth was still intact and that they could become worthy again.

Understanding this principle leads to adequate self-esteem and prevents pride. With humility comes the realization that we are constantly vulnerable. We can all fail completely if we are not careful, as King Benjamin taught: "But this much I can tell you, that if you do not watch yourselves, and your thoughts, and your words, and your deeds, and observe the commandments of God . . . unto the end of your lives, ye must perish. And now, O man, remember, and perish not." (Mosiah 4:30.) Through the Prophet Joseph Smith, the Lord has warned us, "Wherefore let every man beware lest he do that which is not in truth and righteousness before me." (D&C 50:9.)

These concepts can be placed on the codependency continuum as follows:

Selfish	Codependent	Gospel Service
Very low self-worth. Seeks to manipulate those with low self-esteem for his benefit. Worthiness is not valued.	Struggles with self-esteem/self-worth. Has tried to live the "performance-worth" lie. Struggles to maintain feelings of worthiness as it is tied in to the performance of self and others.	Experiences a constant unchanging self-worth. Self-esteem may fluctuate from negative experiences, but self-worth is consistent. Maintaining worthiness is a top priority.

12. We are feeling the benefits of active faith.

Codependents benefit from increased faith especially as they begin to understand the difference between passive and active faith. Our leaders have taught us about this faith.

Hugh B. Brown taught, "Faith is an inescapable necessity in every human life; man cannot do without it because he must take some action with regard to the future. The kind of action taken will depend upon the quality of his faith." (Brown, Hugh B. *Church News*, 4 Jan 1964.) President Gordon B. Hinckley, speaking to the Regional Representatives on 6 April 1984, said, "In all that we do we must cultivate faith. Increased faith is the touchstone to improved church performance." (*Ensign*, May, 1984, p. 99.)

The Prophet Joseph Smith spoke of this faith when he said, "Faith is the assurance which men have of the existence of things which they have not seen, and the principle of action in all intelligent beings . . . What are we to understand by a man's working by faith: . . . we understand that when a man works by faith he works by mental exertion instead of physical force. It is by words, instead of exerting his physical powers, with which every being works when he works by faith." (*Lectures on Faith*, p. 11, 61.)

This active faith heals codependency because it promotes a Christlike service motivated by faith rather than fear. (Codependent service is often motivated by fear.) This type of faith can influence and even change the lives of other people for the better at the same time as it changes the lives of codependents for the better.

Read carefully the following healing scriptures which speak of this faith: "But because of the faith of men he has shown himself unto the world, and glorified the name of the Father, and prepared a way that thereby others might be partakers of the heavenly gift, that they might hope for those things which they have not seen. Wherefore, ye may also have hope, and be partakers of the gift, if ye will but have faith. Behold, it was the faith of Alma and Amulek that caused the prison to tumble to the earth. Behold, it was the faith of Nephi and Lehi that wrought the change upon the Lamanites, that they were baptized with fire and with the Holy Ghost. Behold, it was the faith of Ammon and his brethren which wrought so great a miracle among the Lamanites, (Ether 12:8, 9, 13-15.)

As Ammon's faith led to the wonderful changes in the lives of so many Lamanites, so can our faith be an influence for good in the lives of others. How totally different from codependency is this approach to service, for this approach heals codependency! (For more on faith, see Chapter Four in *The New Stress Reduction for Mormons*.)

13. We no longer enable others.

When we enable someone, we rescue him from the consequences of his behavior and enable him to continue it. As we grow in our healing of codependency, we apply the gospel teaching of free agency and let each person keep personal responsibility and allow them to experience the consequences of their own behavior. We need to let the Spirit guide us so we can find an appropriate balance. It is easy for a recovering codependent to go from the extreme of enabling someone to the other extreme of failing to intervene when appropriate.

14. We are overcoming perfectionism and task orientation.

Perfectionism is a process by which we focus on tasks rather than on feelings. Healing comes as we avoid task-orientation and form healthy, feeling-level relationships with others. When we see building relationships and being loving as more important than getting things done, we are making progress.

15. We are learning how to overcome negatives with positive healthy thinking.

The Apostle Paul taught, "Be not overcome of evil, but overcome evil with good." (Romans 12:21.) This scripture teaches us that we can overcome a negative attribute by focusing in on a positive reality. Spiritual growth can be a positive experience, not a negative one, but for some codependents, their attempts to overcome problems become frustrating and unproductive because their approach to the whole process is negative.

For example, suppose a person wants to overcome the problems of thinking inappropriate thoughts. Trying not to think these thoughts actually feeds the problem, while focusing on positive activities diminishes it.

For example, Julie was troubled with negative thoughts and felt guilty and anxious about them. Every time she tried to stop thinking them, she ended up thinking them more. She concluded that this was happening because she was not trying hard enough to overcome them. Every effort seemed to make the problem worse until she was spending most of her time and energy trying to overcome her negative thoughts.

In desperation, she sought out a therapist, who immediately recognized the futility of her negative approach. He taught her a positive approach by encouraging her to spend the days between appointments reading appropriate books, practicing her musical instrument, helping a friend, memorizing poetry, and preparing for an exam at school. When she returned to the counselor, she reported that she had successfully completed all assignments and had a great week.

Julie didn't understand that *some* problems are best conquered by a positive rather than a negative approach. Still convinced that negatively attacking the problem was the only workable approach, she confronted her therapist, saying she was upset with him because she was paying him good money and they hadn't started working on her problem yet. Like Julie, many of us must gain an awareness of our negative approaches to problems so we can change them and learn to apply Paul's counsel to "overcome evil with good."

As we apply this approach, we need to focus on all three levels of healing: the thought level, the feeling level, and the spiritual level of healing through Christ. This approach is not recommending denial, nor is it interchangeable with the practice of positive thinking. Positive thinking, which some misinterpret as seeing everything from a positive point of view, can actually lead to denying the reality of the situation.

Healthy thinking deals with the reality of a situation, although it may not always be positive. For example, suppose Julie despises rain and wakes up to a severe rainstorm on the day she has planned to have an outdoor picnic. If she responds by saying, "It sure is beautiful outside today. I love rain," she is thinking positively, but she is hardly being honest, and dishonest, positive words are not likely to make her feel better even though they are positive.

If, instead she responds by saying, "I dislike rain, but I can be happy even though it is raining," she is using the skill of healthy thinking. Positive thinking is believing we can do anything even if it is unrealistic, while healthy thinking is believing we can do anything realistic and appropriate for us. (Although great faith can sometimes make the impossible become possible!) A person who is legally blind who decides he must excel in a visual speed-reading course may be thinking positively, but he is not thinking in a healthy or appropriate way. (See "Opportunity Cost" in *Ensign* March, 1978. "How can we make the best decisions," by Neil J. Flinders.)

16. We are learning to avoid the spiritually dangerous codependency trap.

Some people who are in recovery from codependency go too far, from one extreme to the other. It is important to understand the trap of overreaction that can come to a recovering codependent. A person that has been totally self-neglectful in a codependent concern for others can become totally self-centered. A person who has been easily manipulated and overly sensitive to others can become stubborn and insensitive when they overreact.

One woman, named Joan, nearly learned the hard way that trying to overcome codependency can be taken too far. She intensely wanted to end the suffering she had endured in a codependent relationship with her husband. She wrote in her journal: "My codependency began with my need to marry someone who needed fixing. I found someone that fit that description and I married him with a determination to make him into my perfect husband." As she learned about codependency, she was amazed to learn how she had allowed him to control her, and how she had tried to control and fix her husband and her children.

She continued, "I decided to fix what was broken and in the process, I almost broke much more because I decided to divorce my husband. I was angry and I was going to solve my problem. Fortunately, a friend challenged the reasons why I was making my decision. In doing this, my friend prevented me from making a serious mistake. As I drew close to the Lord and became more sensitive to the Spirit, I realized that, for me, I was on an extremely dangerous path. My limited understanding of codependency, combined with my anger, led me to a decision that may not be wrong for every women, but that was very wrong for me. Overreaction is the trap of a recovering codependent; it is important to avoid it."

It is important to understand that the negative attitudes identified earlier on the spiritual growth continuum contribute to the codependency trap! We can avoid this trap with humility and correct knowledge and attitudes. As President Ezra Taft Benson said, "The antidote for pride is humility—meekness, submissiveness. God will have a humble people. Either we will choose to be humble or we can be compelled to be humble." (*Ensign*, May 1989, pp. 6, 7.)

Knowledge of the Lord Jesus Christ and of the healing powers of his gospel come as we become like him. "And this is life eternal, that [we] might know thee, the only true God." (John 17:3.) The only way we can come to know God is to become like him.

17. We are learning to live in the present.

The Apostle Paul taught, "*This* one thing I *do*, forgetting those things which are behind, and reaching forth unto those things which are before." Healing comes when we do "this one thing"—when we leave the past, with our mistakes and sins, behind us so we can enjoy the present and plan for the future with hope.

Because of codependent issues of guilt, some continue to look back and focus on their past mistakes as a way of punishing themselves. Some carry the past as a burden, rather than using it as a learning experience. As someone said, "Let the past instruct, not overwhelm." "When all else is lost, the future still remains." (Bovee.) "The future is ahead—prepare for it. The present is here—live in it." (Monson.)

Part of living in the present includes learning to plan for the future, for as Joseph B. Wirthlin taught, "What people think and believe and plan are all very important, but what they *do* is the thing that counts the most."

18. We are learning to experience the gifts of the Spirit.

The Spirit heals as it purges us of sin and strengthens our weaknesses. Seeking the gifts of the Spirit for the purpose of better serving the Lord also heals, for the Lord said, "But ye are commanded in all things to ask of God . . . [for] that which the Spirit testifies unto you . . . do in all holiness of heart, walking uprightly before me, considering the end of your salvation, doing all things with prayer and thanksgiving, that ye may not be seduced by evil spirits, or doctrines of devils, or the commandments of men. . . seek ye earnestly the best gifts . . . for verily I say unto you, they are given for the benefit of those who love me and keep all my commandments, and him that seeketh so to do; that all may be benefited that seek or that ask of me." (D&C 46:7-9.)

Any of the following are healing gifts from the Lord; as we seek them, we further the healing of our codependency. "To some it is given by the Holy Ghost to know that Jesus Christ is the Son of God, and that he was crucified for the sins of the world. To others it is given to believe on their words, that they might have eternal life if they continue faithful. . . . And again, to some is given the working of miracles; And to others it is given to prophesy; And to others the discerning of spirits. And again, it is given to some to speak with tongues; And to another is given the interpretation of tongues. And all these gifts come from God, for the benefit of the children of God. . . . And it shall come to pass that he that asketh in Spirit shall receive in Spirit; . . . He that asketh in the Spirit asketh according to the will of God; wherefore it is done even as he asketh." (D&C 46: 13-14, 21-26, 28, 30.)

19. We understand the difference between light and works.

The Prophet Joseph Smith taught, "God judges men according to the use they make of the light which He gives them." (TPJS p. 303.) We experience healing as we understand that our light will always be ahead of our works, and we will always have more light than we are presently living. As we increase our works, our light also increases. (Cox, James B. *How to Qualify for the Celestial Kingdom Today.*)

20. We are learning the necessity of receiving the healing grace of the Savior.

Grace is the great gift the Lord gives us when we need help beyond our own means and abilities. It is exactly what the codependent needs in order to be healed. The scriptures teach us that the Savior is "full of grace and truth" (2 Nephi 2: 6); that he is "meek and lowly in heart" (Matthew 11:29); and that "it is by grace that we are saved, after all we can do." (2 Nephi 25:23.) "And if you do these last commandments of mine, which I have given you, the gates of hell shall not prevail against you; for my grace is sufficient for you, and you shall be lifted up at the last day." (D&C 17:8.)

I never understood grace until after I had prayed one evening that the Lord would help me remain faithful and endure to the end. That night I had a dream in which I was climbing a steep hill. I had successfully made it much of the way to the top. I knew if I made it to the top, I would see the Savior and receive the peace that comes after a righteous life. I was thrilled with the possibility of making it to the top of the hill and receiving the rest of the Lord. But as I approached the top of the hill, I was unable to make it the rest of the way. I felt myself slipping. Then I realized that I could not make it on my own, and that only as I *acknowledged* that I could not make it on my own, did I receive the grace and strength I needed *from the Savior* to make it to the top.

We cannot make it back to the Lord without his help. Satan tries to get us to feel guilty about that and think there is something wrong with us. But the Lord wants us to know that this is the plan—that only with the grace of the Lord can we make it. He is always there to help us up the hill. His grace comes as we pray, not only for our own desires, but for the blessings that the Lord knows we need. Consider what the Lord has said about how grace heals us: "Therefore, blessed are they who will repent and hearken unto the voice of the Lord their God; for these are they that shall be saved. And may God grant, in his great fullness, that men might be brought unto repentance and good works, that they might be restored unto grace for grace, according to their works." (Helaman 12:23-24.)

"For by grace are ye saved through faith; and that not of yourselves: *it is* the gift of God: Not of works, lest any man should boast. For we are his workmanship, created in Christ Jesus unto good works, which God hath before ordained that we should walk in them." (Ephesians 2:8-10.)

"Yea, come unto Christ, and be perfected in him, and deny yourselves of all ungodliness; . . . and love God with all your might, mind and strength, then is his grace sufficient for you, that by his grace ye may be perfect in Christ; and if by the grace of God ye are perfect in Christ, ye can in nowise deny the power of God. And again, if ye by the grace of God are perfect in Christ, and deny not his power, then are ye sanctified in Christ by the grace of God, through the shedding of the blood of Christ, which is in the covenant of the Father unto the remission of your sins, that ye become holy, without spot." (Moroni 10:32-33.)

CONCLUSION

I have attempted to plant a few ideas drawn from the scriptures, the writings of Church leaders, and other sources that I felt would promote the healing of codependency. We all need healing in some way. Gospel principles, when lived, promote healing whether we are on the "selfish" end of the codependency continuum or whether we have progressed to the point of "Christlike service." The Prophet Joseph Smith said it best: "May God grant that notwithstanding your great afflictions and sufferings, there may not anything separate us from the love of Christ." (TPJS p. 35.)

The Apostle Paul said, "I have planted, Apollos watered; but God gave the increase." (1 Corinthians 3:6.) The Lord has helped me plant a few ideas that can promote various stages of the healing of codependency. You can nourish these ideas as you prayerfully apply them in your life; however, only God provides the healing. May you experience the healing that comes through the gospel of Jesus Christ that leads people from the bondage of codependency to the freedom and joy of living a Christlike life, feeling his love, and providing Christlike service to others. For "if the Son therefore shall make you free, ye shall be free indeed." (John 8:36.)

About the Author

Dr. John C. Turpin's background is rich in secular and church experience and training. He has earned three university degrees: a Bachelor's degree in education from Weber State University (to teach psychology and history), a Master's degree in guidance and counseling from BYU, and a Doctorate in educational sociology and counseling from the University of Toledo. He has also done post-doctoral work in guidance and counseling at Kent State University.

Dr. Turpin's professional experience includes being an associate professor of education at Baldwin-Wallace College in Ohio for ten years; Director of the Counseling/Psychology Program at the University of Portland; and an educational/management consultant for fifteen years. This has included doing seminars and workshops around the United States largely on the topics of stress-reduction and improving communication skills (and more recently on Codependency). He has spoken for numerous Know Your Religion and BYU Education Week programs for the Church.

His years of helping LDS people in conjunction with his church callings, his work with the Dayspring drug program, and his sincere spiritual and academic preparation give him a wealth of understanding to share.

He and his wife, Barbara have three children: Mike, Jeni, and Laura. They reside in Sandy, Utah. He has served in many church positions and he is currently serving as a counselor to the Sandy Utah East Stake Mission President.